YOGA THEMES
FOR
MODERN YOGIS

YOGA THEMES
FOR
MODERN YOGIS

CONTEMPORARY THEMES, INSPIRATION, TECHNIQUES
& ESSENTIAL GUIDANCE FOR PLANNING
MEANINGFUL & INCLUSIVE
YOGA CLASSES

Madeline Kanuka McGee

Yoga By Madeline

Yoga Themes for Modern Yogis; Contemporary Themes, Inspiration, Techniques & Essential Guidance for Planning Meaningful & Inclusive Yoga Classes

© 2021 Madeline Kanuka McGee, RTY, JD, BA | Yoga By Madeline (YBM). All rights reserved.

First Edition

Includes references and an index.

ISBN: 9798508514198

Imprint: Independently published

No part of this book shall be reproduced, copied, or transmitted by any means, except as premised under the United States Copyright Act.

This book does not contain medical advice. The author makes no warranty with respect to guidance and the author shall not be liable for damages arising therefrom.

Illustrations: created by Madeline Kanuka McGee on Canva.com with edited royalty-free stock images available on Canva.com; Cover art and YBM logo by Madeline Kanuka McGee

Every attempt has been made to appropriately credit individuals for their quotes and content.

For inquiries and feedback, contact media@yogabymadeline.com

Follow YBM on Instagram & other social media platforms @yogabymadeline

www.yogabymadeline.com

For Ruaidhrí

TABLE OF CONTENTS

Foreword by the Author　　　　　　　　　　　　　　　10

INTRODUCTION　　　　　　　　　　　　　　　　　　12

Part One: Class Guidance　　　　　　　　　　　　　　18

PLANNING THEMED CLASSES　　　　　　　　　　　　19

　　Centering Techniques　　　　　　　　　　　　　　20
　　Themed Intentions　　　　　　　　　　　　　　　27
　　Class Preparation　　　　　　　　　　　　　　　29

TABLE OF CONTENTS

Part Two: The Themes	32

I. MINDFULNESS — 33

Conciousness	35
Deceleration	39
Ease	42
Equanimity	46
Focus	50
Presence	54
Serenity	58
Stillness	61
Surrender	65

II. APPRECIATING ABUNDANCE — 69

Beauty	71
Contentment	75
Gratitude	79
Joy	83
Optimism	87
Simplicity	91
Spaciousness	95

III. INVIGORATION — 99

Awakening	100
Creativity	103
Dream	107
Embracing Change	110

Intuition	114

IV. EMPOWERMENT 117

Courage	119
Expansiveness	123
Healing	127
Inner-Flame	130
Patience	134
Perseverance	138
Reassurance	142
Self-Confidence	146

V. INFINITE OPPORTUNITIES 149

Agency	151
Exploration	155
Journey	159
Perspective	162
Positive Habits	166

VI. SELF-APPRECIATION 170

Affirmation	172
Authenticity	176
Life	180
Self-Love	184

TABLE OF CONTENTS

VII. SELF-DISCOVERY — 187

Curiosity	189
Heart-Opening	193
Honesty	196
Integrity	200
Tuning-In	203
Wisdom	207

VIII. BEYOND OURSELVES — 211

Forgiveness	213
Generosity	217
Loving-Kindness	221
Nature & Earth	225
Peace	229
Relationships	233
Selflessness	236
Understanding	239

CONCLUSION — 243

Notes & Other Themes	246
Workbook Pages	253
References & Further Reading	263
Index	265
About the Author	271

Foreword by the Author

When I began my first yoga teacher training course, I was eager to purchase every popular yoga book on the market, believing that these would share the answers for planning perfectly structured and enlightening yoga classes. I envisioned that these books would prepare me for planning classes that would be rich with contemplative themes, challenges, and new experiences. Of course, these were high expectations for books that were not explicitly written for this complex purpose. I also realized that even if a book like this existed, I might quickly exhaust their themes and fall back into a yoga teacher's writers' block. Instead, I needed a book that could inspire me year-round.

When I began planning themed classes, I found myself running out of common yoga philosophy-based themes: the Eight Limbs, the Chakras, lessons from the Bhagavad Gita, and so on. While yoga's rich history and relationship to Eastern medicine are important for all teachers to be familiarized with, these themes also do not always portray what yoga means to each teacher or what the teacher wants to offer their students.

This book began as a personal project to challenge me to plan classes that relate to modern yoga students with a Westernized point of view. As I continued to outline and teach themed classes, I gradually began to incorporate class outlines and self-practice ideas into my compilation of notes. I paired these themes with specific asanas, mindfulness techniques, music, inspirational quotes, and other meaningful elements that link all of us to the essence of yoga through everyday practice.

As my notes grew, I decided to transform them into a book that I can share with other yoga teachers who might appreciate a contemporary perspective on class planning. After all, I had wished this book existed when I began my teaching career and was searching for inspiration and guidance.

My background in writing doctoral-level research papers naturally led me to reference and cite important yoga texts and create an easy-to-reference index in English and Sanskrit. My meticulous teacher training notes have also been a great reference guide and source of inspiration while writing this book.

FOREWARD

This book makes sure not to include step-by-step walkthroughs of classes because I know it is important for authenticity to be represented through class planning and teaching. Instead, this book attempts to make the planning process straightforward. This book also considers how our yoga practice can change day-to-day and acknowledges that we should never be afraid of improvisation and incorporating personal flair. Thus, my hope is that this text inspires yoga teachers to plan unique and thought-provoking classes. Class themes should be selected as they relate to one's life and yoga journey; Thereby, this honest connection and positive energy can inspire students to set meaningful intentions at the start of every class and apply these lessons throughout their own lives.

I am delighted and honored to share this book with the yoga community for the greater purpose of integrating yoga themes that are accessible to all students in yoga's modern age. The themes in this book come from the heart and are genuine to my practice. I tap into my deeper understanding of universal, everyday emotions and experiences that affect and connect all of us.

Light & Love,

Madeline Kanuka McGee

Certified Yoga Instructor | *Yoga By Madeline*

INTRODUCTION

*"Yoga does not just change the way we see things,
it transforms the person who sees."*

– B.K.S. Iyengar

Inspiration for planning yoga classes is all around. In fact, there is so much inspiration that it can be difficult to select a theme for a yoga class. As yoga instructors and practitioners, we might overthink whether a topic is fulfilling enough, too cliché, or rooted so much in yoga philosophy that modern students might struggle to relate to the theme. The purpose of this book is to simplify class planning by presenting themes that everyone can relate to no matter their personal background, yoga experience, or athletic ability.

The yoga themes in this book connect with our ongoing journey as students and teachers through thought-provoking practice themes. To clarify their practical application, this book recommends how to set specific practice intentions that encourage contemplation and instill the importance of continuing to learn more about ourselves in a safe and supportive environment.

This book acts as a foundational toolbox and reference that encourages us to plan meaningful, memorable, and modern classes throughout the years. The fifty-two class themes that are presented highlight our unique yet relatable qualities, while challenging us to learn more about ourselves and grow as individuals on and off of our yoga mats.

INTRODUCTION

This introduction begins by providing an overview of the topics within this book. After, it explains how to approach the themes in this book in order to plan weekly and daily themed yoga classes that resonate with modern yogis, like ourselves.

Overview of Topics

This book is divided into two parts. The temptation might be to jump to the class themes section in the second part of this book, but Part One provides essential guidance on how to apply these themes to your own classes and adapt them to your teaching style and parameters. This information includes an analysis of centering techniques, themed intentions, and class preparation guidelines. This also clarifies the significance of the themes that appear later in this book.

Part Two includes fifty-two yoga themes and classes—enough for every week of the year—that are divided into eight parts and categorized by their overarching topics with their own dedicated chapter. While the themes of Part Two do not need to be read in order, they are categorized by chapter topics that link the themes together and are practical for planning monthly themes and workshops.

Each subdivided theme is paired with an explanation of its significance and recommendations on how to apply these themes to yoga classes. These tips include centering techniques, including meditations, hand gestures, pranayama, and affirmations. The themes are also paired with recommended poses and inspirational material, such as quotes and music suggestions, to help connect themes to other art forms.

Chapter One focuses on Mindfulness themes. This chapter includes class plans for encouraging complete awareness and relaxation in the present moment, and it provides guidance for calming the mind and body through yoga.

Chapter Two includes yoga themes for Appreciating Abundance that already exists within ourselves. These themes help us to recognize *the little things* that happen around us if we learn to pay better attention.

Chapter Three includes themes surrounding the concept of Invigoration. It includes elements of physical awakening through movement and inner-awakening to initiate positive change in our lives. Applying these ideas further, Chapter Four surrounds

Empowerment-related themes that inspire us to reach our full potential and become the best version of ourselves.

Chapter Five includes yoga class themes for recognizing the Infinite Opportunities in our lives. This chapter considers how we can tap into these opportunities by exploring our intrinsic rights and gifted qualities. Similar, but more introspective, Chapter Six is dedicated to Self-Appreciation themes. This class style explores the admirable characteristics that we sometimes overlook.

Chapter Seven includes class themes and plans related to Self-Discovery. Classes of this nature encourage us to learn more about ourselves by opening our hearts and minds to positivity and exploration within ourselves.

Last, Chapter Eight includes class themes that allow us to connect with others and the world as a whole—experiencing what yoga means Beyond Ourselves and aspiring to become one with all living things in the universe.

Before approaching a specific theme, it is suggested that the chapter introductions be read to understand a theme's general significance for this text and its application to the modern yoga practice.

This book also includes a conclusion, references, and suggestions for further reading. You will also find several pages for making personal notes and jotting down class ideas and additional inspiration. Workbook pages are also included that assist in planning additional practice themes using a similar structure that is used throughout the themes of this book. The end of this text contains a useful index for identifying keywords, including poses, meditations, and pranayama techniques. For ease of reference and greater accessibility, Sanskrit translations are also provided.

Approaching the Themes

I recommend applying four simple steps when considering which theme to draw from within this guidebook. First, take notes to express what the theme means to you. Second, select a theme that resonates with you most at a particular time. Third, brainstorm how you would like the theme to be incorporated into a personalized class. This includes considering what you would like to say throughout the class to put the theme into your own words. Fourth, apply and return to a theme. This includes noting what other considerations come to mind, and making additional notes and omissions when you review or rehearse a class.

1. Taking Notes

To help you relate to this guidebook, keep your pencils, pens, highlighters, and sticky notes nearby while you read and reflect. Use these materials to make notes that you can revisit to help you remember how you have connected with each theme in this book. Furthermore, utilize the numerous note sections and margins within this book to make your own theme-inspired notes. Also, use the designated notes pages provided at the end of this book for additional space, and complete the presented workbook pages to plan one-of-a-kind themed classes. Your notes can include personal anecdotes, additional asanas, music, inspirational quotes and readings. Use this book as an integrative journal to advance your yoga journey.

You might also wish to consider how these themes apply to different styles of yoga that you practice or teach. Many of these themes apply across experience levels and styles, including Hatha, Restorative, Vinyasa, and Yin. Allow your ideas to flow. This book provides enough content to unleash your creative mind.

2. Connecting with Themes

While this book surrounds specific themes that are selected based upon their wide applicability to many of us, it is recommended that you select a theme that resonates with you and allows you to teach with sincerity.

The better you can relate to a theme, the better you can explain it to students, and the easier it will be for them to understand and apply the theme to their practice and daily lives. Connecting to a theme also allows us to offer personal anecdotes during class. This encourages vulnerability that establishes a safe space for students. I recommend you practice this simple motto when selecting a yoga class theme: *connect* before you select.

Here is a good two-part test to consider how well you connect with a theme: First, think about how well you can explain it in your own words. And second, consider what you might set as an intention for that practice. If something immediately speaks to you, you might have found a winner for your next class. On the other hand, if your mind begins to drift, you have the choice of revisiting that topic another day, or taking time to understand why you find the theme challenging. You can share that experience with your students to assure them that we can all find a connection and application to our unique lives. After all, yoga in Sanskrit means *union* and to join. Help every student connect and feel like they are part of a supportive community.

3. Class Brainstorming

Once you have selected a class theme that resonates with you or you have envisioned your own, the next step is to begin brainstorming how you would like to adapt the class to your unique teaching style. For this, you might keep a separate brainstorming journal or use loose paper for notes that can be slid between the pages of this book, or use one of the blank pages or workbook pages at the end of this book. Otherwise, you might type your notes if you prefer to keep them digital. Whatever your style, address the following six essential questions and elements:

i. Why does the theme speak to you?

ii. How would you succinctly describe the theme in your own words?

iii. What poses and techniques do you believe represent this theme and why?

iv. What words and phrases would be appropriate to implement during the class? In particular, what would you like to say during movements, during pauses, during challenging elements, and during relaxing parts of the class? This might include writing down synonyms to help prevent too much repetition;

v. Does anything else applicable come to mind? This can include quotes and anecdotes;

vi. Once you create a class plan or rehearse elements of your class, is there anything you would like to add or omit?

Keep your answers nearby as you begin to plan your class, ensuring that you are truly connecting to your class plan and are allowing it to come from your heart. Not to mention, your notes will make the planning process easier than it would be without your own reference.

Following the six brainstorming steps are a guaranteed way to plan a personalized themed class, and should be kept in mind when reading this book. Therefore, I recommend that you refer back to this page throughout your brainstorming process.

4. Applying & Returning

After you teach a class, revisit the margins of your outline and make notes of what worked best and how you might tweak your class in order to teach something similar next time. Encourage your students to provide feedback as well.

If you like a theme, use it throughout the week. After all, this book contains enough themes to allow you to pick a weekly theme all year—and enough recommendations to ensure that each year's themed classes never have to be the same. A theme might also materialize into a running theme over the course of a month of yoga classes, personal practice, or a workshop series. Thus, keep your class notes and plans in your repertoire to revisit. You never need to repeat the same class twice.

Summary

Yoga Themes for Modern Yogis presents an in-depth look at fifty-two yoga class themes that are meaningful and inspiring for today's yoga students. After presenting an overview of this book and offering suggestions on how to approach its themes and advice, this text begins in Part One by presenting essential class guidance for planning classes as it relates to the themes that follow in Part Two. With enough themes to last a lifetime and an abundance of guidance and theme-specific suggestions, this book offers limitless potential for creating rewarding classes for everyone.

Part One
CLASS GUIDANCE

PLANNING THEMED CLASSES

*"Take up one idea... dream of it; think of it; live on that idea.
Let...every part of your body be full of that idea...
this is the way great spiritual giants are produced."*

— Swami Vivekananda

With straightforward themes and a myriad of recommendations, this book intends to spark inspiration and provide direction for planning themed yoga classes for modern yogis. This book is also a practical handbook because it eliminates the difficulty of selecting meaningful themes and planning corresponding classes. In particular, this chapter provides guidance for structuring classes alongside the themes and recommendations of Part Two. As such, this chapter intends to help fill in the blank spaces and utilize allocated class time to its fullest potential—meanwhile, taking into account the various decisions that teachers must make in order to cater a class to their teaching style and authentic voice.

This chapter provides guidance on tailoring and connecting with a class theme by applying centering techniques. It also explains how to encourage students to set a practice intention relating to each theme. Next, this chapter provides guidance for creating step-by-step class outlines that incorporate elements discussed earlier in the chapter. This guidance for planning themed classes will help to create lesson plans with a lasting impact and to inspire students to return to your classes.

Centering Techniques

Yoga class themes should be introduced at the beginning of class and revisited at various points in the practice in both clear and subtle ways. Utilize these opportunities to captivate students' attention and guide them into a contemplative mindset through centering techniques. These techniques include simple mindfulness exercises that keep students focused so that they can find the greatest benefits in their practice. They also reinforce class themes and help students connect with their practice intentions.

This section explores several centering techniques that are common and effective for arriving on the mat and preparing for yoga practice: taking a comfortable position, offering mudra options, leading meditation exercises, teaching pranayama breathing techniques, and offering affirmations. This section also underscores the significance of centering for all classes before these and other similar techniques are revisited in Part Two in relation to specific themes.

Positions for Centering

Settling into comfortable centering positions helps to enter a state of mindfulness and establish a deeper connection with a class theme. Moreover, centering positions help while leading guided meditations and can be used for several minutes at a time. For this reason, it is important to offer position suggestions, including comfortable seated poses and laying-down positions; these can also include the use of props. The following is a list of sitting and reclining centering positions with prop options that assist in leading a themed yoga class:

> Sitting cross-legged on the floor, a block, or a blanket in an *Easy Pose* (Sukhasana);
>
> Sitting on the floor with legs extended in *Seated Staff Pose* (Dandasana), with the option of sitting against a wall and/or placing a bolster or rolled-up pillow under their bent knees;

Sitting in an *Accomplished/Sage Pose* (Siddhasana) with one foot on the floor with the heel coming towards the pelvis and the other heel placed in front of the other;

Sitting on the heels and parallel shins in a *Kneeling Pose* (Vajrasana/Bhujrasana), or kneeling in *Hero Pose* (Virasana) with the seat resting on the floor between the heels—with the optional use of a block or blanket under the hips for added height;

Sitting in *Half Lotus Pose* (Ardha Padmasana), or *Full Lotus Pose* (Padmasana) for students with exceptional hip flexibility, with each foot placed upon the opposite thigh in a crossed-leg fashion;

Sitting against a wall with any of the variations above;

Laying down in *Corpse Pose* (Savasana).

There is no need to incorporate or suggest all of these centering positions, but students should be given select suggestions based on the style of class, their yoga experience, and the class theme. There are no correct positions, but it is important to use discretion in order to make a class feel accessible and comfortable during the most meditative and contemplative parts of class.

Hand Gestures

Hand gestures (*padma mudras*, or simply *mudras*) are another useful centering technique that are frequently used during meditation. These mudras are said to attract specific energies and encourage healing processes. While the Eastern science behind mudras is disputed, they nonetheless act as concentration techniques by offering something to focus on during meditation. For this reason, every theme throughout this book has a suggested mudra that can be used as an optional and accessible centering technique for modern yoga students.

In addition to the specific mudras that are paired with every class theme in this book, this section highlights a few common hand gestures that have wide applicability; These can be used during any meditation and most centering exercises, in addition or instead of those mentioned in Part Two of this book. Three of the most popular mudra options during meditation are Anjali Mudra, Jnana/Gyana Mudra, and Sankalpa Mudra.

Anjali Mudra (sometimes known as *Namaskar Mudra*) is taken to calm and balance our minds and bodies, and to be used as a greeting, such as when we say "Namaste."

> Anjali Mudra is practiced by placing both hands in a prayer position with all ten fingers extended and pressed against one another—meanwhile pressing the thumbs firmly against the heart center.

Jnana Mudra (also spelled Gyana) is common for quiet meditation and helps to experience a grounding sensation. It is also said to grant intuitive knowledge and wisdom.

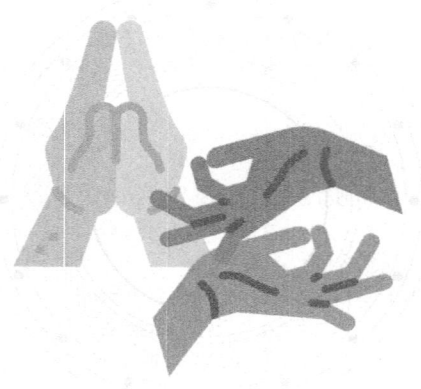

> This mudra involves pressing the index finger and the thumb together in a circular shape while extending the middle, ring, and pinky fingers together.

Sankalpa Mudra is referred to as a Practice Intention Gesture. It is a popular mudra for setting any practice intention if you choose not to incorporate a suggested mudra into a class.

> This is a two-handed mudra. With the right hand, press the tip of the thumb against the inner side of the ring fingernail. With the left hand, take *Akasha Mudra*, which involves pressing the tips of the thumb and middle fingers together.

These three mudras are simple centering techniques but are only a few of numerous hand gestures. For more resources on mudras, view the Additional Resources section of this book.

Guided Meditation Exercises

Meditation can be incorporated into any yoga class as a way to center ourselves and tune into a class theme. It is common to introduce meditation at the beginning of practice and is often used as a recalibrating technique towards the end of a practice. Meditation has countless definitions and unique significance to everyone; In simple terms, meditation is a mindfulness practice that allows us to detach from racing thoughts and emotions, observe our surroundings without judgment, and enter a state of calmness and newfound perspective. As such, guiding students in meditation is an opportunity to help them center themselves and enter a state of mindfulness.

While guided meditation suggestions are offered throughout Part Two of this book concerning specific themes, below are some examples of simple guided meditation exercises that can be practiced and led during any themed class. These specific examples are especially beneficial for students who do not meditate regularly and require guidance.

> Notice which muscles are engaged; Notice which muscles are relaxed;
>
> Notice tastes; Notice smells; Notice sounds;
>
> Notice how the skin feels; Notice where the skin makes contact with clothing, cushions, the floor, or other items;
>
> Notice what colors can be seen through closed eyes;
>
> Conduct a body scan, beginning from the toes to the head while noticing how every individual body part feels; Relax each part one-by-one;
>
> Remain focused on a specific point in your body with every breath, such as the belly or the top of the head;
>
> Notice the temperature of the breath; Notice whether the exhales are warmer than the inhales;
>
> Imagine inhaling a certain color and exhaling a certain color;
>
> Notice whether the breath is shallow or whether the breath is deep;
>
> Count how long each inhale lasts and how long each exhale lasts;

Count down from a certain number and repeat this process until the end of the meditation.

Give students plenty of time to respond to your instructions. Have them notice without judgment or fidgeting. Speak slowly to give them the chance to tune in and enter a more reflective mindset that is so important for a themed class.

Teaching Pranayama

Pranayama refers to breathing techniques and breath control. In Sanskrit, *prana* means breath, life, and energy, and *ayama* means expansion or restraint. As with other centering techniques, pranayama can attract certain energies including calmness or liveliness. Furthermore, we can become relaxed and focused when we pay attention to our breathing and follow a comfortable breathing pattern—allowing us to become more dedicated to class themes and intentions.

While there are various types of pranayama, six of the most popular techniques that suit themed classes are mentioned below: Ujjayi, Sama Vritti, Viloma, Sitali, Nadi Shodhana, and Kapalabhati.

Ujjayi Pranayama, also known as our victorious breath, helps to heighten focus and energize the body throughout flowing yoga practices. For this reason, Ujjayi Pranayama is common in Vinyasa Yoga practice that requires particular attention to pairing breath with movement.

> Ujjayi breathing is practiced by breathing in and out through the nostrils with a slight throat constriction, with attention to fully expanding the lungs and belly. This process imitates the sound of ocean waves.

Sama Vritti Pranayama means equal breathing and helps to reinforce a sense of equilibrium within the body. This form of pranayama requires counting the breath to ensure that inhales are the same length as exhales.

> For Sama Vrtti, practice breathing in and out through the nose. Traditionally, this is done for five-second counts for each even inhale and exhale, however, it is often practiced for any count as long as inhales and exhales are the same length.

Viloma Pranayama means against the hair or grain, and it involves breath retention between inhales and exhales. This helps to focus on being playful with the breath and allowing the mind to become clear of all racing thoughts.

> Viloma can be approached with creativity because the inhales, exhales, and holds can be taken for different counts. There is also the choice of holding the breath after the inhale, after the exhale, or after both. Moreover, Viloma can be paired with other styles of Pranayama by incorporating retention.

Sitali Pranayama means cooling breath, which helps to lower the temperature of the body by breathing out through the mouth using a special technique.

> Sitali breathing involves opening the mouth in a circular shape and curling the tongue either in a straw or taco shell shape, or pressing the underside of the tongue against the backside of the front teeth. Inhale through this shape with a slurpy sound while allowing the breath to hit the back of the throat and exhale through the nostrils.

Nadi Shodhana Pranayama means purifying, or cleansing breath. It is said to purify the nerves, allow the body to feel energized, clear the sinuses, and encourage a balance between the left and right hemispheres of the body and mind.

> Using the right hand, place the index and middle finger between your eyebrows while placing your ring finger on your left nostril. Exhale fully through the left nostril. Inhale through the left and close the left nostril with the thumb. Exhale through the right nostril. Inhale through the right nostril. Close the left nostril with the ring finger and exhale through the left. Repeat this process for 8 to 10 cycles—beginning and ending with the left side.

Kapalabhati Pranayama is known as skull cleansing breath or breath of fire, and it is said to warm up the body and illuminate the mind. This style of pranayama can be difficult to master, so ensure that you are fully comfortable with its technique and demonstration before teaching it to others.

> Kapalabhati involves short and explosive exhales with longer and more passive inhales. These intense exhales are produced by forced lower belly contractions that raise the diaphragm and push air from the lungs.

Sometimes pranayama techniques can cause light-headedness or more serious consequences, so it is imperative to only teach it to others if you have learned it through teacher training or a Guru. Moreover, ask students to consult their doctor before practicing pranayama. You may also consult further references for safety precautions and teaching inspiration, including those listed in the Additional Resources section of this book.

Affirmations

Another important centering technique is to use affirmations. These are repetitive mantras that help to reinforce a positive attribute or thought. They encourage optimism, are a concentration tool for meditation, and reinforce practice intentions for themed classes. For these reasons, every theme within this book is paired with affirmation suggestions that can be shared with students before they repeat the affirmation aloud or in their heads.

There is no correct way to incorporate affirmations, but here is an example suggestion of an affirmation sequence and how it can be incorporated in a class:

> Have students close their eyes and listen while you say an affirmation, such as "I am loved." Pause and have students repeat "I am loved."
>
> From here, you may repeat this process several times, have them repeat this several times to themselves with each breath, or move onto a new affirmation.
>
> Other positive affirmation examples include: "I am important," "I am generous," or "I live a life of abundance." The possibilities are endless.

Affirmations are optional but should tie into the theme of a class to help connect with the theme on a meditative level. Complementing whomever a student dedicated their practice towards, affirmations can be dedicated to oneself, someone else, a group of people, other beings, or something else of personal significance.

Summary of Techniques

The centering techniques addressed in this chapter exist to help all modern yoga students and teachers to enter a state of mindfulness and open-mindedness that is essential during themed yoga classes. Moreover, these techniques can help to reinforce a state of calm and focus before teaching a themed class. The most common of these tools include centering positions, mudras, meditation exercises, pranayama, and affirmations—which were addressed in this chapter and elaborated upon within each theme of this book as they relate to specific topics.

The hope is that this chapter underscores the wide applicability for centering techniques across classes and kindles the continuous learning process as teachers and students.

Themed Intentions

After introducing a class theme how you see fit, it is time to encourage students to set an intention for the practice. While they might already have an intention in mind or prefer to come up with their own dedication for their practice, encourage students to set an intention surrounding the class theme that you have carefully selected. Encouraging specific intentions surrounding a theme can guide students so that they do not overcomplicate the simple task. This process helps all students to feel welcome and understand how they can apply yoga to their everyday lives. This personalized connection to a class theme is another form of centering, mindfulness, and inspiration to constantly learn and grow.

Here is a suggested six-part sequence for guiding students in setting their themed intentions at the beginning of a yoga practice:

    i.   After an introduction and optional centering techniques, ask students to bring their palms together and extend the fingers upwards, as if to pray, and press their thumbs firmly against their heart (Anjali/Namaskar Mudra). This is a common mudra to incorporate during the intention-setting portion of a class because it helps to connect with one's emotions, equilibrium, meditative state, and contemplative mindset;

ii. Ask students to bow and connect their forehead to their hands—connecting their heart and mind;

iii. Provide at least one example to help guide students in focusing their minds on the task of intention-setting;

iv. Ask students to consider how the theme resonates with them and encourage them to set an intention surrounding what comes to mind. You might also mention that they are welcome to set any other intention that they would like, adding that they should make this practice their own;

v. Pause for several seconds to allow students to reflect on their intention and how it connects to the overall class theme;

vi. When students are ready, they may raise their heads and release their hands.

By following these or similar steps, students will have the opportunity to carefully consider their practice intentions and dedicate their practice towards something or someone that is important to them. Taking the time to encourage intention-setting can also help students better connect to a yoga class theme and apply it to their practice and everyday lives.

After encouraging students to set an intention, plan how you would like to transition into the next part of the practice however you see fit. Here are some examples of what you can guide students to do next:

Have students leave their hands on their thighs for a moment to maintain a mindful state. Ask them to let go of anything that no longer serves them, and ensure them that their body and mind are at ease. Tell them to let go of any worries; If something is important enough, it will come back to them after class. Be present in the time they have dedicated to themselves;

You might incorporate centering techniques, such as those highlighted earlier in this chapter, or those paired with the themes in Part Two. In particular, affirmations are useful for sealing a thought and reinforcing an intention.

There is no correct way to encourage intention-setting, but these steps help to create a smooth transition between introducing a theme and proceeding with the rest of a themed class. This process also pairs with the intention sections for each theme in Part Two.

Students should feel comfortable to set any intention they would like—although themed intentions can help students to better connect with the lessons you intend to share and can help them better understand how yoga can apply to their everyday lives.

Class Preparation

After deciding on a practice theme, appropriate centering techniques, and how you would like to guide your students on setting a class intention, it is time to plan the class structure. This section addresses how to plan a yoga class in two straightforward steps: first, by creating a comprehensive class outline, and second, by establishing and following personalized pre-class considerations. These steps act as guidance that can be adjusted to any teaching style and parameters.

Class Outline

The first step of planning a themed yoga class is by creating an outline by breaking down the stages of your class. Below is an exemplary themed class plan outline that can be paired with the suggestions throughout this book to simplify the planning process. This nine-step example can be adjusted to fit the length and style of any class.

   i. Open the class with a greeting, before explaining the type of class and asking if students have any injuries if they have not told you about it already. Ask students to take a comfortable seat and close down their eyes. With eyes closed for confidentiality, ask students to raise their hand if they would prefer not to receive adjustments;

   ii. Drawing from this book's suggestions, conduct any brief introductory centering and mindfulness technique(s) of your choice. This allows students to mindfully enter the room;

iii. Introduce the class theme with help from the overviews in this book. Explain the theme and give examples, including a possible personal anecdote and selected quotes;

iv. Seal the intention through any other centering technique(s), such as those already paired with each theme in Part Two;

v. Warm up the class with initial easy movements to awaken the joints, muscles, and tune into the breath;

vi. Lead students down your planned pathway towards peak poses, such as those suggested in Part Two while incorporating any necessary warming up and stretching;

vii. Explain and demonstrate any peak poses before guiding students into the asanas. This is a good time to remind them of their intentions;

viii. Wind down the class by taking any counter-movements and slowing down the pace as you work towards the final resting position;

ix. Conclude the class with any other centering techniques, suggested quotes, songs and readings, and a personalized closing in your authentic voice.

After creating a class plan, you can reference it as an example for future classes. You can also follow these steps to create a personalized class template that you can adapt to any theme. In both circumstances, you have created a plan that you can revisit, tweak, and continue to use throughout your yoga teaching career.

Additional Considerations

Before teaching, some additional class considerations are helpful to keep in mind. These include checklists for class preparation, class promotion, remembering what to bring, and setting up.

After you have planned your class, run through the class on your mat to make sure you are comfortable teaching the positions, that you have accounted for adequate preparation for the asanas with modifications, and your transitions flow into one another. Then, transfer your notes into a journal that you can keep with you for reference at any time during the class. Notes demonstrate to students that you have put significant thought into what you are teaching—especially when you are basing the class around a well-prepared theme with supporting materials.

Consider promoting your classes online using a website and social media. With a class or weekly theme in mind, you can give a quote or a short description suggested alongside the themes in Part Two. This is also a way to stay connected to your existing and future students and prepare them for class and its theme. Allow it to resonate with them throughout the day and week, even as they scroll through modern devices.

Make a checklist for what you would like to bring to class. There are obvious things, like a yoga mat and your notes, but there are other things that might slip from your mind. Bring a water bottle, a way to keep track of time (such as a silent watch alarm, a sand timer, or a clock that does not distract students), a speaker (if the studio does not have one), a way to play music (such as a laptop), reading materials (like a book for poems or an excerpt), and a tripod if you are recording or live-streaming the class.

Give yourself plenty of time to set up for class. Roll out your mat, set up your music, have your class plan open, and take a few minutes for your own centering and mindfulness. When you feel at ease, you can use any extra time for warming up and waiting to greet your students as they walk into the practice space. Remember to connect with students through eye contact and by remembering their names and little things about them.

These additional considerations are suggestions based upon my own experience, and I encourage you to make personalized checklists that suit your own teaching style and goals.

Class Preparation Summary

Well-thought-out themed yoga classes in our modern era require a class outline and staying true to your evolving style. That said, do not stress over any part of the process or worry that a class does not tie in enough with a theme. Trust in your confidence and improvisation skills, and consider all of the recommendations in Part Two so that you always have enough content to offer a rewarding, thought-provoking, and memorable class for your students.

Part Two

THE THEMES

I. MINDFULNESS

"Mindfulness practice means that we commit fully in each moment to be present... in full awareness, with the intention to embody... an orientation of calmness, mindfulness, and equanimity right here and right now."

— Jon Kabat-Zinn

Once yoga mats are unrolled and students are comfortable, it is time to tune into the present moment. Let all worries drift away, clear the mind, and know that important thoughts that flow through modern yogis' minds will return after class.

This chapter is inspired by this spirit of calm that is incorporated at the beginning of yoga classes; It presents yoga class themes that embrace being *here and now*. This refers to being mindfully engaged and captivated by the present moment and observing our current circumstances and surroundings with objectivity. Accordingly, this chapter includes nine class themes and extensive inspiration for planning mindfulness-based classes. These are Consciousness, Deceleration, Ease, Equanimity, Focus, Presence, Serenity, Stillness, and Surrender.

The theme of *Consciousness* allows us to notice without judgment in order to detach from the stresses of life. *Deceleration* allows us to become more relaxed in a busy world. *Ease* encourages us to find comfort at any moment. *Equanimity* helps to bring balance into our lives. *Focus* helps us to realize our priorities. *Presence* allows us to appreciate the immediate moment. *Serenity* helps to bring tranquility in any setting. *Stillness* brings a busy mind to a halt. And *Surrender* allows us to release all tension.

Each of these mindfulness-related themes is explored with the use of explanations, centering exercises, asana suggestions, and inspirational material. This section offers enough content to plan several months' worth of meaningful and mindful yoga classes that connect with the modern yogi.

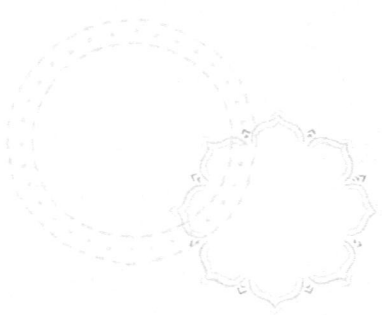

Consciousness

Consciousness means to be aware; It is about tuning into surroundings, appreciating the present moment, and being cognizant of oneself.

Yoga practice integrates the concept of consciousness physically, emotionally, and mindfully. Every breath, movement, and moment of stillness should be practiced with conscious intention. Thus, incorporating consciousness as a yoga class theme allows students to connect with this fundamental element of yoga that threads through every class and personal practice session.

Specifically, consciousness can be practiced through mindful thoughts and movement. It involves tuning into our breathing, taking note of our senses, and paying close attention to what our mind and body are saying at any particular moment. It is working towards becoming divinely aware and in tune with ourselves and our surroundings. Thus, a class on consciousness should incorporate these essential elements in order to have students find peace and acceptance within themselves.

Consciousness as an Intention

Encourage students to set an intention surrounding how they can be more conscious of something in their lives. This could be as fundamental as being more cognizant and appreciative of the present moment. Consciousness might also relate to a specific person, the outdoors, health, or something else that might be overlooked and underappreciated in their lives. Allow this theme to shape students' intentions and inspire their practice by becoming more aware and appreciative of everything that they are able to experience.

Consciousness in Mindfulness Practice

To tap into a state of consciousness, begin in *Chin Mudra* (Unrestricted Consciousness Gesture), which is believed to encourage calmness and peace with all surroundings in order to enter a more meditative state.

> With each hand, extend the pinky, ring, and index fingers, while slightly curling the index finger under the thumb. Keep the palms upward and rest the back of the palms on the knees.

Holding Chin Mudra, have students repeat the following affirmations:

> *I am at peace with my surroundings; I am mindful of the world around me; I acknowledge my inner-calm; I appreciate what deserves my attention;* etc.

Lead a guided *body scan* meditation, beginning from the tip of the head, down to the toes—objectively noting how every part of the body feels. You might also wish to notice each of the five senses one-by-one.

Review *Ujjayi Pranayama* to encourage consciousness of this style of breathing that is required throughout asana practice. Becoming more conscious of the breath can also relax the body and enter a more focused state of mind

Consciousness in Asana Practice

Dedicate plenty of time in sitting, kneeling, and other meditation-friendly positions to focus on all sensations in and around the body. Options include *Lotus Pose* (Padmasana), *Hero Pose* (Virasana), *Kneeling Pose* (Vajrasana/Bhujrasana) while sitting on the heels or props, Seated *Staff Pose* (Dandasana) with extended legs, and *Sage Pose* (Siddhasana) in a simple cross-legged position or similar variation with or without props.

You can also consider spending time meditating in relaxation poses such as *Child's Pose* (Balasana), *Reclining Hero Pose* (Supta Virasana), *Reclined Butterfly Pose* (Supta Baddha Konasana), *Supported Bridge* (Salamba Setu Bandha Sarvangasana), and *Corpse Pose* (Savasana).

Throughout the entirety of the practice, take more time than usual to break down the particulars of common and peak asanas by explaining exactly how they should be aligned, and what students should be feeling in specific parts of their body. Encourage them to be conscious of every moment.

More Inspiration on Consciousness

"We are one blink away from being fully awake." — Pema Chodron

"The world is full of magic things, patiently waiting for our senses to grow sharper." — W.B. Yeats

"The aim of life is to live, and to live means to be aware, joyously, drunkenly, serenely, divinely aware." — Henry Miller

"Until you make the unconscious conscious, it will direct your life and you will call it fate." — C.G. Jung

"There is a presence, a silence, a stillness which is here by itself. There is no doer of it, no creator of this stillness. It is simply here in you, with you. It is the fragrance of your own self. There is nothing to do about this, it is naturally present. This fragrance of peace, this spaciousness, it is the fragrance of your own being." — Mooji

"The ability to observe without evaluating is the highest form of intelligence." — Jiddu Krishnamurti

- ♪ *Open Awareness* – Denean
- ♪ *Consciousness Meditation* – Chinmaya Dunster
- ♪ *Clarity* – Sarah Watson

YOGA THEMES FOR MODERN YOGIS

Notes

Deceleration

Deceleration is the act of slowing down. It involves becoming less active and more relaxed. This applies to us in a physical sense, such as when we slow down after exercise or in a car when a stoplight turns yellow. Deceleration is also experienced psychologically as it relates to a slowing-down of our thoughts. This is significant when thoughts, stresses, and movement around us encourages a racing mind.

Slowing down through yoga can mean a literal deceleration of the heartbeat, breath, and rate of movement. As such, the physical and mental experience of deceleration can help us tap into our parasympathetic nervous system, thereby experiencing a calmer state, lowering stress levels, and preventing fight-or-flight responses.

Deceleration as an Intention

Allow students to take a moment to consider how they have recently experienced a racing mind. Give examples, such as juggling several tasks, overreacting to something that was out of their control, or having worries about a future event.

Encourage students to set an intention surrounding how they can experience deceleration in their life in order to enter a calm state, whereby everything seems easier and goals seem attainable through incremental tasks. In doing so, the act of slowing down also allows us to better appreciate and enjoy more of the beautiful things around us—to take more time to smell the flowers. Meanwhile, a deceleration-themed intention reinforces a more relaxed state that is better equipped to respond to everyday stresses.

Deceleration in Mindfulness Practice

During meditation, lead students into *Mahashirsha Mudra* (Overactive Mind Relief Gesture), which helps to decelerate a busy mind.

To take this mudra, tuck the ring finger into the palm center, extend the pinky finger, and pinch the thumb, middle, and index fingers together.

Once in Mahashirsha Mudra, ask students to repeat the following affirmations:

Time is on my side; It is okay for me to slow down; I have time to appreciate the little things; The best things take time; etc.

As a pranayama exercise, guide students in making their exhales longer than inhales. For example, have them breathe in for a count of two and exhale for a count of four. Elongating the exhale can allow our heart rate and breathing to slow down, thereby acting as a relaxation breathing technique.

Deceleration Through Asana

Child's Pose (Balasana) is one of the most effective asanas for allowing us to slow down our breathing and heart rate. You may wish to elongate exhales when holding this pose for several breaths—keeping the head grounded and the hips pulling down towards the heels.

To experience deceleration through movement, you might try slowing down a *Sun Salutation* (Surya Namaskar), rather than taking a quick Vinyasa flow. Move with intention and steady breathing while noticing every minuscule transfer of weight and every tiny muscle activation. Stay in *Downward-Facing Dog* (Adho Mukha Svanasana) for at least five breaths each time to tune into how the body is feeling. Understand and appreciate the complexity and achievement that the body experiences when it slows down.

More Inspiration on Deceleration

"Slow and steady wins the race."– Aesop

MINDFULNESS

"The day you stop racing, is the day you win the race." – Bob Marley

"A mind that is racing over worries about the future or recycling resentments from the past is ill-equipped to handle the challenges of the moment. By slowing down, we can train the mind to focus completely in the present. Then we will find that we can function well whatever the difficulties. That is what it means to be stress-proof: not avoiding stress but being at our best under pressure, calm, cool, and creative in the midst of the storm." – Eknath Easwaran

"Never be in a hurry; do everything quietly and in a calm spirit. Do not lose your inner peace for anything whatsoever, even if your whole world seems upset." – Saint Francis de Sales

"In this media-drenched, multitasking, always-on age, many of us have forgotten how to unplug and immerse ourselves completely in the moment. We have forgotten how to slow down. Not surprisingly, this fast-forward culture is taking a toll on everything from our diet and health to our work and the environment." – Carl Honoré

- ♪ *Crown of Amber Canopy* – Slow Meadow
- ♪ *Reversed Stress* – Minonna
- ♪ *Stillness is Waiting* – Alex Couture

Notes

Ease

Ease is a state without difficulty, stress, effort, unpleasantness, or pain. Ease is about letting things be and trusting that everything will be okay. It involves feeling content, comfortable, and relaxed in the present moment.

Exploring the theme of ease in modern yoga classes helps to alleviate stress and function with clear and conscious minds. Tapping into our ease element requires us to become more mindful and to slow down our thoughts and physical movements—practices that can be performed and improved through yoga.

Ease as an Intention

Allow students to consider what elements in their life they wish would become easier. Provide examples such as working towards a goal, a healing process, or lingering stress. Maybe students think of several examples, but encourage them to focus on one specific element. Ask them to set an intention to find contentment and ease despite any discomfort they might feel when confronting this element.

By being specific with their intentions, students can avoid overwhelming emotions that can arise when thinking about several issues at once. Instead, students can practice compartmentalizing issues in their lives in order to address them consecutively and experience a calmer mindset with lasting ease.

Ease in Mindfulness Practice

Lead students into *Sukham Mudra* (Stress-Relief Gesture), which encourages deceleration and alleviates stress to avoid exhaustion due to an overactive mind.

> This mudra is practiced on both hands, by pressing the thumbs onto the nails of the pinky fingers.

Have students practice elongating their exhales to come into a deeper relaxation before focusing on equal breathing (Sama Vritti Pranayama). Have students count to three they inhale and count to three as they exhale to find evenness of breath and find comfort in their natural breathing patterns.

Optional affirmations related to ease include the following:

> *My body and mind are at ease; I release all stress and become blissful; Everything is easier when I am at ease;* etc.

Ease Through Asana

We can consciously practice a sense of ease by pausing during peak poses where effort is greatest. At these points, ask students to find a level of comfort. This can be paired with repeating an affirmation or telling an inspirational quote in order to encourage a sense of ease. You can also have students focus on their breathing and notice how poses become easier as they correct their alignment and engage the proper muscles.

Also, reinforce the importance of finding ease in *Downward-Facing Dog* (Adho Mukha Svanasana) so that students can find relaxation when pausing in this active pose. This way, students will be able to tune back into their breath and find a sense of calm before completing a flowing series of poses.

Similar to Doward-Facing Dog, focus on finding ease in *Dolphin Pose* (Ardha Pincha Mayurasana). This asana can release excess tension along the calf muscles and help to find rest while activating the core and arm engagement. Finding ease in Dolphin Pose can also train students to develop the strength and comfort that is required for more challenging inversions, such as *Headstand* (Sirsasana).

You might also consider taking *Reclining Hero Pose* (Supta Virasana) variations, gradually working from an upright *Hero* (Virasana) towards full Hero on the back, or on supporting bolsters or blankets. Hero can be a very intense pose so encourage students to use as many props as they need in order to feel at ease during a challenging asana.

More Inspiration for Ease

"Respond from the center of the hurricane, rather than reacting from the chaos of the storm." – George Mumford

"If you want to conquer the anxiety of life, live in the moment, live in the breath." – Amit Ray

"How wild it was to let it be." – Cheryl Strayed

"Learning to let go should be learned before learning to get. Life should be touched, not strangled. You've got to relax, let it happen at times, and at others move forward with it." – Ray Bradbury

"Step back. Allow things to unfold. There's a beauty to be found in letting things be." – Tamara Levitt

"Your ability to generate power is directly proportional to your ability to relax." – David Allen

"The more relaxed you are, the better you are at everything." – Bill Murray

- ♪ *Lullaby* – Sarah Watson
- ♪ *Calm* – Govinda
- ♪ *Restful* – Ifeelu
- ♪ *The Calm* — Dream Runner

MINDFULNESS

Notes

Equanimity

Equanimity is an evenness of mind and body, through a balance of effort and ease. Experiencing a state of equanimity allows us to find clarity when making decisions and appreciating the present moment.

Yoga also relates to equanimity because it involves a balance between effort and ease—but we sometimes need a reminder to work towards this balance. Tapping into a state of equanimity can allow us to approach more difficult asanas through a new lens—training our minds to also approach more challenging tasks throughout our lives with additional comfort, calmness, and clarity.

Equanimity as an Intention

Ask students to consider how they would like to experience greater balance in their lives. For example, they might be spending a significant amount of time on a particular task despite wanting to spend time on something they enjoy or needing to dedicate time to something they have avoided. Ask them to set an intention surrounding how they would like to find more equanimity in this area or a similar area in their life.

A yoga class surrounding equanimity can help to practice an evenness of mind and a balance between effort and ease. By focusing on this theme, students can tap into the state of mind that will allow them to experience this sense of equanimity in additional areas of their life and encourage them to make their intention a reality.

Mindful Equanimity

Ask students to take *Samasti Mudra* (Integrating Brain Hemispheres Gesture), which is said to balance the brain hemispheres and allow them to communicate effectively.

This mudra is done by making a peace sign shape with the hands, with the thumb pushing down the pinking and ring fingers towards the palm, while extending the pointer and middle fingers.

While maintaining Samasti Mudra, consider having students repeat equanimity-themed affirmations like the following:

My mind and body are in perfect balance; I am a harmonious being ; I find equanimity at this moment; etc.

Pranayama can also help us tap into a state of equanimity. In particular, practice equal breathing (Sama Vritti) by counting to an even number with each inhale and the same even number with each exhale. This can help students find equanimity in the rhythm of their breath. This exercise also encourages a state of balance between effort and ease by finding comfort while controlling the breath.

You can also pair equal breathing with other pranayama techniques such as alternate nostril breathing (Nadi Shodhana). In this case, have students place their pointer finger under their nose while breathing out through each nostril, noticing whether more air is escaping from their right or left nostril. Have students note a possible imbalance. Practice at least 8 rounds of Nadi Shodhana before trying the same breath test with the index finger. After the breathing exercise, notice how air more evenly escapes from each nostril.

Equanimity Through Asana

To practice equanimity through asana practice, mirror what each side of the body has done, and pay special attention to incorporating counterposes and repeating any poses or flows with the same technique on each side.

Moreover, the concept of equanimity should be explained during comfortable seated positions that have a mirrored left and right side, such as *Lotus Pose* (Padmasana) and *Accomplished/Sage Pose* (Siddhasana). These positions represent equanimity by having each side of the body in equilibrium in addition to offering a comfortable meditative position that can allow students to better reflect on equanimity within their minds.

Another simple way to practice equanimity is by noticing the spinal curves and shoulder blade movements when transitioning between *Cat Pose* (Marjaryasana) and *Cow Pose* (Bitilasana). These movements and counter-movements can help us understand our capacity to adapt to the ebbs and flows of life. After, feel a neutralized and long spine in *Tabletop Pose* (Bharmanasana).

Another example of how to practice equanimity is by incorporating a *Dancing Warrior* flow into a Vinyasa class. This flow is based on *Sun Salutation B* (Surya Namaskar B) and includes *Warrior Two* (Virabhadrasana II), Reverse/Exalted Warrior (Viparita Virabhadrasana), and *Extended Side-Angle* Pose (Utthita Parsvakonasana). Have students pay special attention to each flowing movement to ensure they balance their left and right sides. Meanwhile, have students notice how the muscles and other tissues find balance as they work simultaneously and experience equanimity. Have students also notice whether one side might be stronger or more flexible than the other, and let the goal of equanimity allow each side of your body to be a teacher for the other and find harmony together.

Inspiration on Equanimity

"Equanimity is the hallmark of spirituality. It is neither chasing nor avoiding but just being in the middle." — Amit Ray

"You have control over doing your respective duty, but no control or claim over the result. Fear of failure, from being emotionally attached to the fruit of work, is the greatest impediment to success because it robs efficiency by constantly disturbing the equanimity of mind." — Ramananda Prasad

"Equanimity is inner smoothness." — Jeff Warren

"A modern definition of equanimity: cool. This refers to one whose mind remains stable & calm in all situations." — Allan Lokos

♪ *Soothe* — Alan Ellis

MINDFULNESS

♪ *Somewhere in Between* – August Wilhelmsson
♪ *Equal* – Dylan Francis

Notes

Focus

Focus means to be engaged and concentrated on a particular point, or to have directed attention. It also requires dedication and full attention, which are essential for completing tasks and improving efficiency. Moreover, our character and life can be shaped by what we pay attention to because our focus shapes our perspective and influences our decisions.

In yoga, focus allows us to concentrate on proper alignment and balance in asana practice, and allows us to calm a racing mind during meditation. This required focus also strengthens our capacity to concentrate on important tasks after a yoga class concludes. Thus, a yoga class surrounding the theme of focus helps modern students apply lessons of yoga in practical ways and helps them avoid the temptation of distractions and procrastination in their daily lives. Students are also given the opportunity to practice focusing on what matters and will benefit themselves and others.

Focus as an Intention

Explain to students that this class intends to exercise attention skills. In doing so, they can strengthen their sense of focus and direction in their everyday lives. In this vein, have students consider what they might have struggled to focus on recently. This might be a project, a goal, studies, the needs of someone else, or any simple tasks such as becoming a better listener.

Then, encourage students to set an intention to improve their focus—whether that is general or relates to something specific. As such, allow this practice to strengthen their ability to pay better attention to what matters most on and off of the yoga mat. Have them continue to revisit and focus on this intention throughout the class.

Mindfulness for Focusing

Take *Ajna Mudra* (Brow Chakra/Third Eye Gesture), for focusing attention, clarifying the mind, and improving concentration. This mudra involves both hands.

> Clasp the left hand into a light fist and extend the pointer finger; With the right hand, make a fist around the left pointer finger.

To continue centering, consider offering the following affirmations for focusing:

> *I focus my mind; I concentrate my attention on positive elements of my life; My focus determines my destiny; I take time to appreciate what is in front of me*; etc.

Practice a *home base* meditation, which is to focus on one particular thing (the home base) throughout the meditation. Begin by guiding your students on focusing on their breath. Have them imagine a part of their body that is affected by the breath, such as the belly or throat, and remain focused on that point as a home base to keep their attention fixed.

After practicing this breath-focused home base meditation for several breaths or minutes, challenge students to find another home base, such as a different body part, a sense, or something around them. This meditation can last as long as you see fit and it can be revisited towards the end of practice to recenter.

Focus Through Asana

Practice balancing positions to challenge and strengthen our sense of focus that is required to remain calm and stable. These asanas can include standing balances, like *Tree Pose* (Vrksasana) with the lifted foot resting above or below the standing leg knee. Other options include *Eagle Pose* (Garudasana) with the arms and legs wrapped, and Toe Stand (Padangusthasana) with the lifted leg in a figure-four positioning over the standing leg's thigh. Focus can also be challenged through arm balances, such as *Crow/Crane Pose*

(Bakasana) with different variations, and *Scorpion Pose* (Vrischikasana) for more advanced students.

Before entering these focusing-themed poses, explain the concept of a *Drishti* (eye gaze) to students. Have them select a non-moving point in front of them to focus on before slowly raising any part of the body from the ground. Detract their attention from moving objects and wobbling neighbors. To challenge their focus further, have them close their eyes and continue to imagine the same still point ahead of them or a new point of focus within themselves.

Inspiration for Focus

"[Y]our focus determines your reality." – George Lucas

"Focus on your strengths, not your weaknesses. / Focus on your character, not your reputation. / Focus on your blessings, not your misfortunes." – Roy T. Bennett

"The real secret of life is to be completely engaged with what you are doing in the here and now." – Alan Watts

"It is during our darkest moments that we must focus to see the light." – Aristotle

"You can't depend on your eyes when your imagination is out of focus." – Mark Twain

"We can always choose to perceive things differently. We can focus on what's wrong in our life, or we can focus on what's right." – Marianne Williamson

"What you stay focused on will grow." – Roy T. Bennett

Escaping Time – Benjamin Martins

- ♪ *Focus* – Light of Sun
- ♪ *Celeste* – Pete Kuzma

MINDFULNESS

Notes

Presence

To be present is to be completely focused on what someone is experiencing at a particular moment. Presence encourages awareness and receptivity. It is objective and indifferent to the past and the future, and it only lives in the actual moment.

Presence helps to prevent our minds from wandering while practicing meditation, and it allows us to stay focused and centered during yoga practice. For this reason, exercising our ability to be truly present through yoga is similar to practicing mindfulness, whereby the current moment is noted and cherished.

Presence as an Intention

Remind students to let go of all worries and be fully present before setting an intention. They have made time to attend class and should appreciate every moment that they have dedicated to themselves.

Allow students to consider ways that they might wish they were more present. For example, this could relate to being present for someone that they have a relationship with, or for something that they are not giving adequate care to. Depending on what comes to mind, have students set an intention surrounding how they can be more present.

Throughout the class, students should focus on being present during every moment on the mat and should be willing to strengthen their mindfulness toolbox. As such, these practices can inspire them to be more present in their everyday lives and the lives of their loved ones.

Practicing Presence through Mindfulness

Take *Dhyana Mudra* (Meditation Gesture), which provides calming energy for meditation, deep contemplation, and reflection. It also allows us to reach our full potential.

> For this mudra, simply place an opened right hand with the palm upwards on top of an opened left hand with that palm also facing upwards, as if to receive a small offering from someone. Then, touch the tips of the thumbs together to create a triangle shape within the outlines of the thumbs and index fingers.

Holding the mudra, have students repeat presence-themed affirmations, such as the following examples:

> *My past has no bearing on my present; I enjoy every moment; This moment is a gift; I honor the present with my full* attention; I am here; I am now; I am present and aware; etc.

For additional centering, guide students in a *home base* meditation by selecting one particular thing in the room and have them focus on that with objectivity. After, ask students to change their home base to a part of themselves, such as their breath, a body part, or colors that they imagine as they breathe or visualize through closed eyelids. Have students find this home base within themselves, thereby appreciating the present moment within.

Presence Through Asanas

Take *Seated Staff Pose* (Dandasana). This asana can heighten our sense of presence by experiencing a seated position that still requires strong muscle engagement throughout the body. Have students pay attention to how the body reacts to each minute element of the pose and how the ground feels underneath them in the present moment—rather than simply sitting with extended legs and letting the mind wander. To feel contact with the ground, some students

might place blocks under their hands or tent their fingertips on the ground beside their hips to draw their shoulders up, back, and towards one another.

You might also consider one-legged balancing positions that require heightened concentration and presence in order to remain steady. Examples include *Tree Pose* (Vrksasana), *Eagle Pose* (Garudasana), and *Bird of Paradise* (Svarga Dvijasana), whereby students must focus on a *Drishti* (a point of focus).

Inspiration on Presence

"The past has no power over the present moment." – Eckhart Tolle

"This time, like all times, is a very good one, if we but know what to do with it." – Ralph Waldo Emerson

"Make the present moment your friend rather than your enemy." – Dan Harris

"Presence is the ground of compassion." – Jeff Warren

"If you are depressed you are living in the past / if you are anxious you are living in the future / if you are at peace, you are living in the present." – Lao Tzu

"If you want to be happy, do not dwell in the past, do not worry about the future, focus on living fully in the present." – Roy T. Bennett

"Realize deeply that the present moment is all you have. Make the NOW the primary focus of your life." – Eckhart Tolle

"Just become aware of your breath, and through that come into the present moment, where everyday activities can take on a joyful miraculous quality." – Thich Nhat Hanh

- ♪ The Consolations of Philosophy – Max Richter
- ♪ *Presence* – Ty Burhoe, Bill Douglas, Amy Ippoliti
- ♪ *Boy 1904* – Jónsi, Alex Somers

MINDFULNESS

Notes

Serenity

Experiencing serenity involves feeling calmness, peacefulness, and tranquility. The body and mind are untroubled and at complete ease. Serenity is free from disturbance and it nurtures a gentle inner-joy.

Yoga can help us to experience serenity by finding bliss in the present moment. We can seek serenity through yoga by exercising our ability to accept current circumstances, respect ourselves, and find peace in our surroundings. By embracing these elements in a modern yoga class, we can enter a serene mindset that outlasts the practice.

Serenity as an Intention

Encourage students to release all worries and refrain from considering any stresses in their lives. The beginning of this practice requires a complete sense of bliss in order to achieve and cherish serenity throughout the class. Tap into this positivity and have students dedicate their practice to heightening their ability to experience and appreciate serenity, and to strengthen their serene and tranquil awareness in various circumstances.

Serenity through Mindfulness

Have students settle into a position that they find most comfortable at the time, whether that is sitting or reclined. Have students consider how their selection is one of their bodies' ways of understanding serenity in the current moment.

Begin by challenging students to feel serenity within the room. Notice the calmness in the air, in the sounds around them, and within themselves. Have them note how this makes them feel. For further centering, practice a similar meditation that explores the *five senses* as they relate to students' surroundings and notice the experience of serenity with every sensation. This heightens the body's ability to recognize and embrace serenity in everyday moments.

Have students take *Sahasrara Mudra* (Thousand-Petalled Lotus Gesture), which calms the spirit, encourages awareness of life's spiritual dimension and activates the body's self-healing power.

> Practice this two-handed mudra by extending and splaying the fingers from each hand, while touching the tips of the thumbs together and tips of the index fingers together—creating a triangle shape between the hands.

Maintaining a comfortable position and the mudra, have students repeat affirmations as a way to maintain serene awareness:

> *I am at complete ease; I experience tranquility; I find serenity in my surroundings; My mind and body are at peace;* etc.

Pause after mantras are repeated for a few rounds and have students sink deeper into a state of calm and serenity.

Serenity through Asana

Serenity can be experienced in *Reclined Butterfly Pose* (Supta Baddha Konasana), which releases physical and emotional tension that is held within the hips. For added comfort or something new to try, place blocks or rolled blankets under the knees; Notice how this added support can help to feel more comfortable and to relax deeper into the hip stretch.

Serenity can also be experienced in other positions that allow us to feel our calmest. These include Restorative Yoga positions, such as a deeply relaxing *Corpse Pose* (Savasana) and a calming *Child's Pose* (Balasana). In these positions, allow every muscle to relax while the body sinks lower into the earth below.

More Inspiration on Serenity

"We are not going to change the whole world, but we can change ourselves and feel free as birds. We can be serene even in the midst of calamities and, by our serenity, make others more tranquil. Serenity is contagious." — Swami Satchidananda

"Each person deserves a day away in which no problems are confronted, no solutions searched for." — Maya Angelou

"Every breath we take, every step we make, can be filled with peace, joy and serenity." — Thich Nhat Hanh

"When even one virtue becomes our nature, the mind becomes clean and tranquil. Then there is no need to practice meditation; we will automatically be meditating always." — Swami Satchidananda

- ♪ *Escape Gravity* — Juni Tinley
- ♪ *Serenity of Touch* — Niigata
- ♪ *Song of Bliss* — OSLEE

Notes

Stillness

Stillness is to abstain from motion in body or mind. It is to pause in a world that is in continual motion, find beauty in what happens in the current moment, and observe how the world works in complex ways that are greater than ourselves.

Stillness relates to yoga because it provides opportunities to be more cognizant of our surroundings and be more aware of our relation to the world. As such, a practice dedicated to the theme of stillness underscores the importance of embracing more conscientiousness throughout our lives.

Stillness is the second of three Yin Yoga principles; The first being to find a variation of a pose that is appropriate for your body at a given time, and the third being to stay awhile after finding a place to stay. Thus, stillness in yoga represents a way to discover deeper benefits of poses that might not be as appreciated if positions are only held for brief moments. The same goes for centering and mindfulness techniques, whereby the longer we dedicate to stillness during the practice, the further we can enter a meditative state, and the greater the benefits will be for our minds and bodies. Therefore, stillness is an appropriate theme for modern yoga students who are interested in deepening their mindfulness practice.

Stillness as an Intention

Ask students to release any racing thoughts and bring the mind to complete stillness. Assure them that the constant movement of life and the continuous rotation of earth do not mean that we need to move as well. Have them take the seat of the observer and ask them to consider how stillness might bring them more peace and calm. Then, encourage students to set an intention surrounding how they would like to apply more stillness to their lives.

Stillness Through Mindfulness

Have students take any comfortable position while sitting or lying down and ask students not to fidget during meditation and commit to a position. For encouragement, you might read inspirational quotes and poems about the benefits of stillness.

For an added element of stillness, have students take *Bhairava Mudra*. This hand gesture assists with inner reflection and destroys the ego, thereby also allowing for a greater appreciation of the world around us.

> Bhairava Mudra requires placing an upward-facing open right hand (for masculine energy) on top of an open left hand. Another option is to place the left hand on top instead, representing female energy.

While in the mudra, have students repeat affirmations like the following:

> *I allow myself to experience stillness; I allow myself to do absolutely nothing at this moment; I stay still amidst a world of constant movement*; etc.

Furthermore, consider having students practice *breath retention* (Viloma Pranayama) by holding the breath for a moment at the top of each deep inhale, and holding the breath for a moment at the bottom of each full exhale. With each pause in the breath, ask students to notice complete stillness within themselves—particularly in their ribcage, belly, and mind. Repeat this process for several rounds of breath before coming to a natural breathing pattern and maintaining the sensations of inner-stillness.

Stillness through Asana

To practice stillness in asana practice, have students pause in *Downward-Facing Dog* (Adho Mukha Svanasana) and *Child's Pose* (Balasana) at various parts of the class for several breaths at a time. These two asanas should be treated as resting positions to return to stillness and students' intentions.

Similarly, lead a meditation in the final resting position, *Corpse Pose* (Savasana), at the end of class that reinforces the theme of stillness. Encourage students to remain still by imagining a heavy blanket draping over them, sinking them into the ground. Another variation involves having students place sandbags on their shoulders and thighs to glue them onto the floor and keep the body still with the use of props.

For a challenge, have students come to complete stillness during balancing positions, such as *Standing Extended-Leg* Stretch (Utthita Hasta Padangusthasana). Have them focus on a non-moving point ahead to help the body remain still. Explain how stillness within our surroundings encourages stillness within ourselves.

Inspiration on Stillness

"The stiller we get, the deeper we go." – Jeff Warren

"Learning how to be still, to really be still and let life happen – that stillness becomes a radiance." – Morgan Freeman

"In the midst of movement and chaos, keep stillness inside of you." – Deepak Chopra

"When everything is moving and shifting, the only way to counteract chaos is stillness. When things feel extraordinary, strive for ordinary. When the surface is wavy, dive deeper for quieter waters." – Kristin Armstrong

"In the stillness of your presence, you can feel your own formless and timeless reality as the unmanifested life that animates your physical form. You can then feel the same life deep within every other human and every other creature. You look beyond the veil of form and separation. This is the realization of oneness. This is love." – Eckhart Tolle

"When you don't know what to do, do nothing. Be still." – Oprah Winfrey

"To a mind that is still the whole universe surrenders." – Lao Tzu

♪ *Be Still* – The Fray
♪ *River* – Hiatus

YOGA THEMES FOR MODERN YOGIS

♪ *Still* – Bombay Bicycle Club
♪ *Still Moment* – Tunde Jegede

Notes

Surrender

Surrendering means to stop trying to prevent or control thoughts, experiences, tension, and emotions. It involves giving into current circumstances and letting go of all effort.

Surrendering does not necessarily mean giving up; Rather, it means that we no longer battle the difficulties around us. Surrender is a way to experience peace as long as we are willing to experience it.

The concept of surrender is often practiced in Yin Yoga, where we can achieve the greatest benefits of deep stretching when we completely commit and surrender into a position. The simultaneous discomfort and deep release help us relieve tension that might not otherwise escape from a brief stretch that is held for just a few breaths. Thus, by choosing to surrender in yoga, we experience a renewed sense of release and a feeling of self-induced tranquility.

Surrender as an Intention

Allow students to consider what is causing tension in their lives and have them dedicate their practice to surrendering and breathing into those feelings, rather than fighting them. You might provide examples, such as physical tension, relationship strains, or stress relating to something beyond control. Allow them to set an intention to simply surrender and let go of anything holding them back from peace and calmness.

Centering for Surrender

Have students take *Uttarabodhi II/Ksepana Mudra* (Letting Go Gesture). This is believed to encourage feelings of joy and freedom while releasing negative energy. It allows the body to feel light and grounded simultaneously. This allows us to surrender with ease

To take this mudra, clasp both hands together with the left thumb crossed over the right thumb, and both index fingers extending together.

Maintaining the mudra, have students repeat affirmations such as the following:

I release all stress and let go; nothing is holding me back; I surrender to gravity; I completely relax; I am at ease; etc.

For further centering, guide students through a *body scan* meditation to have them notice where they would like to relieve physical tension. When they come to a spot that feels achy or tight, encourage them to stay for a few deep breaths through the nose and sighing exhales through the mouth to surrender to the sensation. Have them imagine exhaling discomfort and whatever might be holding them back, and surrendering into the calmness of the practice space with each inhale.

Surrender through Asana

The theme of surrender is especially represented by Yin and Restorative positions. In Yin Yoga, the surrender into stretches can release the fascia that connects the body's tissues, while nurturing the parasympathetic nervous system. In Restorative Yoga, we allow the body to remain still and surrender into a comfortable position variation to help heal the body.

For example, our capacity to surrender can be challenged through deep hip and glute stretches such as *Low Lizard* (Utthan Pristhasana), also known as *Dragon Pose* in Yin. Another example is *Pigeon Pose* (Eka Pada Rajakapotasana), also known as *Swan Pose* in Yin Yoga. Both of these poses can be held for extended periods of time while bodyweight allows the hip flexors to expand and surrender.

Students can also grant their bodies an opportunity to surrender down the spine by taking a simple forward fold from a *Standing Forward Bend* (Uttanasana) or *Rag Doll* variation with bent knees. After staying for a while, pause to have students notice alleviated tension in different parts of their bodies—exemplifying the holistic benefits of surrender beyond a single stretch.

Further, *Corpse Pose* (Savasana) represents the ultimate expression of physical and mental surrender. Allow students to experiment in Savasana with different props—such as blankets, bolsters, blocks, straps, and sandbags to find a position that they can surrender into comfortably. Students can remain here for up to twenty minutes to fully marinate in the pose.

Additional Inspiration on Surrender

"Try something different. Surrender." – Rumi

"Surrender is a journey from the outer turmoil to the inner peace." – Sri Chinmoy

"Instead of resisting to changes, surrender. Let life be with you, not against you. If you think 'My life will be upside down' don't worry. How do you know down is not better than upside?" – Shams Tabrizi

"Always say 'yes' to the present moment. What could be more futile, more insane, than to create inner resistance to what already is? What could be more insane than to oppose life itself, which is now and always now? Surrender to what is. Say 'yes' to life — and see how life suddenly starts working for you rather than against you." – Eckhart Tolle

"By giving up the need to know, we can begin to know in a whole new way." – Shinzen Young

- ♪ *Helpless* – Buffy Sainte-Marie
- ♪ *I Release Control* – Alexa Sunshine Rose
- ♪ *Sunshine* – Cello Version, Limelight Glow
- ♪ *Closing Meditation* – Shantala

YOGA THEMES FOR MODERN YOGIS

Notes

II. APPRECIATING ABUNDANCE

*"Abundance is not something we acquire.
It is something we tune into"*

— Wayne Dyer

Our human nature often drives us to desire more than what we have, but yoga reminds us of the wonderful qualities and possessions that we already have. Yoga allows us to be content and appreciative of our lives as they are. Accordingly, this chapter includes modern yoga class themes surrounding how we can apply yoga as an instrument for recognizing and enjoying the abundance that exists in our daily lives.

This chapter contains seven essential class themes that encourage us to appreciate abundance: Beauty, Contentment, Gratitude, Joy, Optimism, Simplicity, and Spaciousness.

The theme of *Beauty* relates to appreciating this quality beyond its superficial definition. *Contentment* regards how we can be at ease and fulfilled by our current circumstances. A theme on *Gratitude* relates to being thankful for what we have. The theme of *Joy* allows us to find happiness at any moment. An *Optimism* theme encourages us to practice a more positive outlook on life. *Simplicity* as a theme helps us to appreciate ordinary things that we might otherwise overlook. And *Spaciousness* is addressed in a literal and figurative sense—helping us to recognize our ability to expand within a world that can make us feel confined. By applying this chapter's themes to classes and our personal practice, yoga can help us appreciate our abundance on and off of the mat.

Each of these abundance-related themes is addressed with introductory explanations, centering techniques, position suggestions, and additional thought-provoking content—presenting limitless inspiration for modern yoga classes.

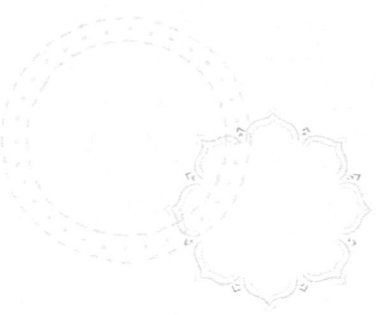

Beauty

Beauty describes something or someone with certain qualities that make it or them undeniably attractive. Often, beauty is used as a synonym for aesthetically pretty and pleasing, but the compliment has a deeper complexity that cannot be seen. Beauty involves countless peripheral elements, including our other senses and our greater understanding of background, personality, authenticity, wisdom, and unique qualities.

Yoga reveals the beauty within ourselves and encourages a greater appreciation of others far beyond the superficial definition of beauty. It honors the beauty of everyone by adapting poses to suit all bodies and embracing everyone's genuine selves. We honor the beauty of nature by naming poses after plants and animals, and we honor culture by naming poses after legendary figures. Yoga embodies the complex definition of beauty that gives us a greater appreciation of the world.

Beauty as an Intention

Have students consider what beauty means to them in an abstract sense. Next, have them think about something they find beautiful about themselves. If their mind leads them towards negative traits, challenge them to find beauty in whatever it is that comes to mind. Offer examples of beautiful qualities and character traits, such as kindness, compassion, wisdom, and curiosity.

Encourage students to set an intention to see beauty in imperfections and to become more appreciative of the true beauty that surrounds them.

Beauty Through Centering

To assist students in centering, have them sit in a comfortable variation of *Lotus Pose* (Padmasana) to achieve symmetry on their left and right sides, with hips open like a lotus flower floating on water. Complimenting students' choice of a lotus-inspired seated position, have them take *Padma Mudra* (Lotus Mudra or Flower Mudra), which also symbolizes a beautiful budded lotus flower that rises from mud and murky water. This mudra also represents that beauty is beyond aesthetics and there is more to know than what we see at face value.

> Practice this two-handed mudra by touching the base of the palms together, the tips of the pinkies together, and the tips of the thumbs together. Then, peel the index, middle, and ring fingers away from one another while exposing the inside of the palms to the sky. This creates the shape of a lotus flower.

Holding Padma Mudra, have students repeat affirmations for beauty, such as the following:

> *I see beauty in everything; beauty is around me; beauty is within me; I am beautiful; I see imperfections as beauty; beauty exists wherever I go; Wherever I go, beauty follows;* etc.

Furthermore, lead students in a *day trip* meditation by asking them to close their eyes and imagine themselves somewhere beautiful—whether this is a place from their memory or imagined altogether. Have them consider what they see from different views and how this vision sounds, smells and feels. After marinating in this daydream, have them consider why this place is so beautiful to them. This can help to understand our internal perception of beauty and appreciation for the world.

Beauty in Asana

Encompass a wide definition of beauty by exploring poses with stories and complexities behind their names. For example, *King Dancer Pose* (Natarajasana) is a picturesque and universally beautiful pose. It requires challenges for balancing, stretching, and strengthening that represent the intricacy of the asana's beauty.

APPRECIATING ABUNDANCE

Dancer Pose also has an ancient story; It is named after Shiva, the patron deity of art and yoga, and the first yoga practitioner and teacher. Thus, Dancer Pose can be said to honor yoga itself and everything beautiful that it represents.

Another asana to incorporate is *Mermaid Pose*, which is named after the beautiful and mythological half-human-half-fish that the pose is named after. Mermaid Pose is a variation of King Pigeon Pose (Eka Pada Rajakapotasana) that includes a twist while hooking the back foot into the crease of the same size elbow while clasping both hands. Mermaid pose is also appropriate to include as a warm-up before King Dancer Pose because both poses involve similar and beautiful intricacies.

Inspiration on Beauty

"Everyone has beauty; but not everyone sees it." – Confucius

"Even the stones placed in one's path can be made into something beautiful." – Goethe

"We are all wonderful, beautiful wrecks. That's what connects us—that we're all broken, all beautifully imperfect." – Emilio Estevez

"Sometimes people are beautiful. Not in looks. Not in what they say. Just in what they are." – Markus Zusak

"Think of all the beauty still left around you and be happy." – Anne Frank

- ♪ *Beautiful Calm* – Johann Eder
- ♪ *You are so Beautiful* – Charles Lloyd, Norah Jones
- ♪ *What a Wonderful World* – Katie Melua, Eva Cassidy

YOGA THEMES FOR MODERN YOGIS

Notes

Contentment

In its simplest sense, contentment relates to being at peace with what we have. Contentment is important to practice because we can easily continue wanting more than what we have, even when those things are not necessary or practical. And sometimes the attainment of these desires does not fill the void or make us feel the way we had anticipated. These lusts are often for material things but can include desired characteristics for ourselves—pulling us away from achieving a content and happy life.

Practicing contentment through yoga can help us to live more appreciative lives by finding abundance through a wiser mindset that is always available to us if we wish to access it. Contentment also relates to the traditional yoga theme of *Santosha*, which embodies the concepts of contentment and self-acceptance. Thus, focusing a class on the theme of contentment can help yogis to break down their understanding of Santosha in a modern light.

Contentment as an Intention

Allow students to reflect on the role of contentment in their lives. Recognize that we might be distracted by thoughts of things that we want or things want to get rid of; Acknowledge those thoughts and allow them to drift away.

Encourage students to set an intention surrounding contentment by considering how they can be more at ease and appreciative of what they have. Allow that intention to set a mindset of contentment throughout the practice so that the skill can be exercised and applied in practical ways.

Centering for Contentment

Take *Vyana Mudra* (Expansive Prana Gesture) that has various layers that tap into our subtle energy and meditative mindset. It helps to open the heart, live harmoniously with others, reduce tension, and encourage calmness.

> Take this mudra by ticking the nail of the index finger under the thumb's underside. Then, touch the tips of the index finger and thumbs together while gently extending the pinky.

Maintaining Vyana Mudra, have students repeat affirmations such as the following:

> *I am happy where I am today; I am at ease; I am content here and now; I have everything I need; I have enough; I will not let myself have too much;* etc.

For an accompanying meditation, lead students in a *memory trip* visualization exercise. Allow them to imagine a time that they were truly content. Have them consider the details of that moment and smile. Hang onto that feeling throughout the practice.

Contentment through Asana

Explore the concept of contentment through accepting and honoring their level of flexibility in sitting and standing forward bends. For example, have students transition from *Seated-Staff Pose* (Dandasana) into an accessible variation of a Seated Forward Bend (Paschimottanasana). Perhaps bent or supported knees offer more comfortable variations of the pose, or perhaps students prefer to reach somewhere along the shins or reach behind the feet to grab a wrist.

Another forward bend option is taking a *Standing Forward Fold* (Uttanasana) with bent or straightened knees while focusing on bending at the hips. Students can also release deeper into the fold by clasping the hands behind the back and drawing them over the head. Students might also grab the heels to pull themselves closer to their shins.

These forward bends represent contentment because flexibility can vary day-to-day and at different times, while also sometimes taking years to reach the deepest expression of the poses. Our facia and other tissues run from our feet and up the length of our spine, giving everyone plenty of space to accumulate tension.

No matter where a student reaches or how they modify a forward fold, remind them to keep a long back and be content with wherever they reach. There is always room to improve and be critical—but there is also plenty of room to be grateful, appreciative and content. This practice allows us to feel happy within ourselves and inspire us to keep returning to the mat.

For more, you might consider other basic poses with different variations and opportunities to notice our individual anatomy and how we are feeling on a specific day. Or, you might consider asanas that trigger frustration in order to challenge us more to find contentment during difficult or unhappy times.

More Inspiration on Contentment

"I am a lover of what is, not because I'm a spiritual person, but because it hurts when I argue with reality." – Byron Katie

"You have power over your mind – not outside events. / Realize this and you will find strength." – Marcus Aurelius

"Do not spoil what you have by desiring what you have not; remember that what you now have was once among the things you only hoped for." – Epicurus

"If you could accept that perfection is impossible what would you stop obsessing over?" – Rupi Kaur

- ♪ *Looking Forward, Looking Backward* – Robin Bennich
- ♪ *I am Everything* – Beautiful Chorus
- ♪ *River* – Leon Bridges
- ♪ *I Am What I Am* – Aykanna

YOGA THEMES FOR MODERN YOGIS

Notes

Gratitude

Gratitude is the state of being grateful. It is defined as expressing deep appreciation, thankfulness, and contentment. Gratitude requires the absence of desire in order to appreciate what we already have and build the foundation for happiness that is free from ego and self-discouragement.

Gratitude also represents the yogic concept of *Santosha*, which is translated as "contentment" from Sanskrit. To practice Santosha, we must practice being humble, thankful, and satisfied. By doing so, we can feel at ease and grateful for what we have. A way to guide us in this positive direction is by practicing the theme of gratitude as a yoga theme.

Gratitude as an Intention

Allow students to imagine being completely content with what they have; not wanting anything more and not being jealous of anyone. Let them reflect on how that makes them feel about themselves.

Provide some examples of gratitude; This might include health, family, friendship, shelter, love, opportunities, etc. In that mindset, help students consider what they are most grateful for, what they think they should be more grateful for, or ways that they would like to express their gratitude. Have students build an intention around that person or element.

Centering for Gratitude

Take *Anjali Mudra* (My Essence Meets Your Essence Gesture), which represents a sign of gratitude, devotion, and humility. This mudra is also sometimes referred to as the *Namaste* position because the mudra carries the same meaning as this Sanskrit word.

To take this mudra, place your hands in a prayer position with the palms pressed together and fingers extended. Draw the thumbs towards the heart center and press against the ribs.

Have students repeat affirmations like the following:

I have enough, I have everything I need; Everything I desire is within me; I appreciate the people and gifts that surround me; Abundance flows through me; I am safe and all is well; etc.

Practicing pranayama, have students visualize themselves inhaling gratefulness and exhaling to release any negative feelings. To be more specific, one exhale can be dedicated to releasing jealousy and another to releasing selfishness. Inhales can be dedicated to family, friends, and health. Play with the breath in this way.

Gratitude through Asana

In all poses during this practice, inspire students to find gratefulness in what they can accomplish, rather than focusing on what is difficult or how they are hoping to look. An example of how to do this is by incorporating inspirational quotes throughout the practice, and especially during peak poses and centering—keeping the mind focused on gratitude.

Sticking to simpler asanas and *Sun Salutation* (Surya Namaskar) poses can help to reinforce what students can do rather than highlighting what they might not be able to achieve. Give modifications for all poses and allow students to select their variations with gratitude and their full dedication. For example, suggest *Cobra Pose* (Bhujangasana) instead of *Upward-Facing Dog Pose* (Urdhva Mukha Svanasana), *Child's Pose* (Balasana) instead of *Downward-Facing Dog Pose* (Adho Mukha Svanasana), and bending the knees enough in a *Standing Forward Fold* (Uttanasana) so that the torso touches the thighs. Have students feel gratitude for every movement their bodies are capable of doing.

More Inspiration on Gratitude

"A grateful mind is a great mind which eventually attracts great things." – Plato

"Think of what you have rather than what you lack. Of the things you have, select the best and then reflect how eagerly you would have sought them if you did not have them." – Marcus Aurelius

"Stop thinking gratitude is a by-product of your circumstances and start thinking of it as a world view." – Bryan Robes

"Gratitude builds a bridge to abundance." – Roy T. Bennett

"I dive into the well of my body... everything I need already exists in me..." – Rupi Kaur

"I would maintain that thanks are the highest form of thought; and that gratitude is happiness doubled by wonder." – G.K. Chesterton

"Gratitude makes sense of our past, brings peace for today; and creates a vision for tomorrow." – Melody Beattie

"Life is not measured by the number of breaths we take, but by the moments that take our breath away." – Maya Angelou

"Feeling gratitude and not expressing it is like wrapping a gift and not giving it." – William Arthur Ward

- ♪ *Grateful Minds* – Mehdi Teyt & Rehla X
- ♪ *Gratitude* – chillchild
- ♪ Bountiful Blissful And Beautiful – Kamari & Manvir

YOGA THEMES FOR MODERN YOGIS

Notes

Joy

Joy describes utmost happiness and the experience of delight, which is simple and pure. We can experience joy every day if we open our hearts and minds to recognizing it—appreciating beauty in day-to-day experiences and taking moments to reflect upon our wellbeing and achievements.

Joy can be experienced in modern yoga classes by acknowledging and encouraging happiness with every breath and movement. Like yoga, a natural state of joy is unassuming, unadulterated, and honest in expression.

Joy as an Intention

To bring about a joyful state of mind, have students imagine feelings of joy. Have students consider what brings them joy—whether this is something they have experienced for a while or something that has happened to them recently that has evoked joy. Have them hold that feeling close to their hearts and allow that joy to fuel a positive practice. Encourage students to set an intention to embrace joy through yoga and their daily lives.

Centering for Joy

Have students take *Udana Mudra* (Upward-Flying Energy Gesture), which encourages self-expression, joy, lightness, and laughter.

> To take this mudra, press the tips of the thumb and index fingers together, then press the finger pad of the middle finger into the nail of the index finger and slightly extend the ring and pinky fingers.

Consider having students repeat joy-inspired affirmations, such as the following:

My natural state is joyful; I am truly happy; I experience joy in this moment: I am filled with happiness and joy; etc.

Lead students a simple meditation where they smile with every inhale that guides the crown of the head and creases of the lips towards the sky. With every exhale, let out an audible and joyful sigh. Repeat this for several rounds.

You might also guide students in a dynamic breathing exercise by standing in a wide-leg stance and having students raise their arms above their heads. Take a deep breath to inflate the lungs before having students swing their arms and body into a dynamic wide-leg *Forward Fold* (Uttanasana) with arms and heads released towards the ground. With a smile, release with a relaxing 'ahh' sound. Repeat this exercise a few times to help initiate joy and positive energy. Ensure students initiate the bend at their hips to protect their spines.

Joy through Asana

Joy is represented through *Cobra Pose* (Bhujangasana) and its deeper variations of Seal Pose (Salamba Bhujangasana), and *Upward-Facing Dog* (Urdhva Mukha Svanasana). These positions open our hearts and naturally guide our lips into a smile. They can also be incorporated into Vinyasa sequences while experiencing joy flowing like water throughout our bodies.

Also consider deeper heart-opening positions, including *Dancer Pose* (Natarajasana) to experience a similar sense of joy as the heart peels open.

Joy can also be reinforced during challenging poses including other backbends like *Wheel/Upward Bow Pose* (Urdhva Dhanurasana). In these poses, students should not push themselves past a point of joy. If joy is not present, this is an indication that it is time to lessen the intensity or skip a pose altogether.

In addition, joy can be experienced through asana by being playful with movements. This allows us to take variations and free movement to encourage happiness through self-expression at any particular moment.

More Inspiration on Joy

"Happiness is closer to the experience of acceptance and contentment than it is to pleasure. True happiness exists as the spacious and compassionate heart's willingness to feel whatever is present." — Noah Levine

"Happiness is not to be sought outside. It can never come from outside or from inside--because it simply is. It is always. Where? Everywhere." — Swami Satchidananda

"Very little is needed to make a happy life./ It is within yourself, in your / way of thinking." — Marcus Aurelius

"Happiness is a state of inner fulfilment, not the gratification of inexhaustible desire for outward things." — Matthieu Ricard.

"For every minute you are angry; you lose sixty seconds of happiness." — Ralph Waldo Emerson

"Happiness is part of who we are. Joy is the feeling" — Tony DeLiso

"There is no path to happiness. Happiness is the path." — Gautama Buddha

"If we smile at someone, he or she will smile back. And a smile costs nothing. We should plague everyone with joy. If we are to die in a minute, why not die happily, laughing?" — Swami Satchidananda

- ♪ *Chime* — Alan Gogoll
- ♪ *In the Light* — The Lumineers
- ♪ *I Am Happy* — Snatam Kaur

YOGA THEMES FOR MODERN YOGIS

Notes

Optimism

Optimism is a state of positivity, hopefulness, and anticipation of future successes. Practicing optimism involves recognizing what is good, right, just, and beautiful around us. It allows us to see possibilities everywhere. By contrast, a state of pessimism involves the tendency to see the bad and negative sides of people and things around us; Pessimists see obstacles when optimists see opportunity.

Yoga represents optimism by helping us to continue recognizing the little successes and progressions towards expressing the full version of an asana and strengthening our mindfulness practice. A state of optimism also creates a positive atmosphere for all students that encourages growth and inspires future goals of modern yogis.

Optimism as an Intention

Have students consider something worrying or challenging in their life and have them dedicate their practice towards focusing on optimism. Students can also set a general intention to practice more optimism throughout each day. Allow their intentions to help train their minds to appreciate unanticipated changes and serendipitous moments that are unavoidable throughout life.

Centering for Optimism

Practice *Sankalpa Mudra* (Practice Intention Gesture), which helps to create positive imagery, and inspire goals and freedom of expression. Thus, Sankalpa Mudra encourages optimism in the present and future.

> Beginning with the right hand, rest the tip of the thumb on the left part of the ring finger's nail. Then with the left hand, bring the tips of the thumb and middle finger together (in *Akash mudra*).

In Sankalpa Mudra, ask students to repeat affirmations for optimism, such as the following:

> *I am filled with enthusiasm for life; I focus on progress; Today is a great day; I am lucky; Things always work out well for me; Hope and love surround me; Optimism flows through me; I am prepared for any challenge;* etc.

For additional centering, lead students in a *day trip* meditation, having them imagine their future in the best possible light. Have them consider what they will be doing and how they will be living. And have them consider how this makes them feel. Then, have them consider having control in achieving this future, and that they are capable of a positive outcome.

Optimism through Asana

Select a peak pose, or several peak poses that will be especially challenging for your students. After preparing students for the asana(s), demonstrating how to safely enter and exit the pose. Explain how repeated practice is required to be able to take the asana in its full expression, before allowing students to try the pose. As you observe, remind students to be optimistic and focus on progress from the day before, last week, last year, or even at the beginning of class. If it is their first attempting the pose, explain how they have already accomplished an impressive challenge that will only become easier. Remind students that with practice, they will continue to improve their technique.

A challenging asana that represents optimism is *Bird of Paradise* (Svarga Dvijasana), whereby students will eventually open up from a flower bud into an exotic flower that the pose is named after. Modifications include simply working on the bind, or keeping a bent lifted leg as they rise.

Another asana that represents optimism is *Yogi Squat/Garland Pose* (Malasana). To work towards the full expression with optimism, some students might wish to sit on a block or widen their stance. They can also take twists while opening one hand to the sky—opening the chest, and guiding the hips open before repeating this on the opposite side. Gradually, the hips will continue to open, the sit bones will continue to lower, and the heart will lift towards the sky.

Further, some students might practice jumping from *Crane/Crow Pose* (Bakasana) into *Low Plank* (Chaturanga) as a challenging transition. Draw students back to their intentions to help them experience a sense of optimism, rejoice in what they can achieve, and imagine what they can achieve in the near future.

More Inspiration on Optimism

"A great attitude becomes a great day which becomes a great month which becomes a great year which becomes a great life." – Mandy Hale

"Remember that sometimes not getting what you want is a wonderful stroke of luck." – Dalai Lama

"We must accept finite disappointment, but we must never lose infinite hope." – Martin Luther King

"The pessimist sees difficulty in every opportunity. The optimist sees the opportunity in every difficulty." – Winston Churchill

"How wonderful it is that nobody need wait a single moment before starting to improve the world." – Anne Frank

- ♪ *Angels Prayer* – Ty Burhoe, James Hoskins, Cat McCarthy
- ♪ *Afterglow (Acoustic)* – Wilkinson, Becky Hill
- ♪ *breathe again* – Joy Oladokun

YOGA THEMES FOR MODERN YOGIS

Notes

Simplicity

Simplicity is a quality or fact that something is uncomplicated, ordinary, or natural. It is unadorned and has no unnecessary elements. While simplicity sometimes has a negative connotation because it suggests plainness, the purity and vulnerability of simplicity make it undeniably beautiful. After all, *the little things* make us the happiest.

Yoga can seem intimidating to new yogis, but after a short while, every student begins to embrace repetition of movement and realize the practice is only as complicated as they would like to make it. Yogis realize that the philosophically complex art of yoga is more straightforward and simpler than previously imagined. At the fundamental level, yoga helps us feel good and achieve a modern version of enlightenment.

Simplicity as an Intention

Let students consider an element of their life that they consider simple and unelaborate, yet also undesirable because of these characteristics. Have students think about why they feel that way and have them highlight why simplicity actually makes this element beautiful.

After, take a minute to consider something else in their life that is beautiful because it is simple. You can give them examples such as a memory of an act of kindness, spending time with a significant other or a child's first steps, or any living thing that they love. It might even be something innate about themselves that they love.

Ask students how they feel after that exercise and encourage them to set an intention of appreciating the simpler things in their lives. This can be broad, or relate to something in particular that they might have underappreciated the simplicity of.

Centering for Simplicity

Lead students into *Hamsasya Mudra* (Swan's Face Gesture), which is an artistic expression symbolizing the picking of a flower in the curiosity of its smell, or to place in one's hair. This mudra has a childlike simplicity by representing how beauty can be found in tiny gestures. It can also represent accomplishing tasks and making decisions.

> To take this mudra, press the thumb underneath a flattened and horizontal index finger. Splay the middle, ring, and little fingers upwards.

To reinforce the beauty of simplicity and its practical understanding, consider having students repeat affirmations such as the following:

> *I find comfort in the little things; I appreciate the beauty in simplicity; I have what I need; I rejoice in the simplicity of life*; etc.

Furthermore, lead students in reviewing *Ujjayi* Pranayama—one of the most simple and foundational yoga breathing techniques that helps to calm the mind and feel energized throughout practice. As you break down the technique, highlight its complexities and numerous benefits.

Simplicity through Asana

Low Crescent Lunge (Anjaneyasana) represents simplicity and its positive attributes because of its potential for various forms of expression. Low Crescent Pose is often incorporated into beginners' classes and introduced as a warm-up towards the beginning of other classes because it acts as a simple but essential foundation from which students' practices can grow.

With simple alterations, Low Crescent can transition into *Low Lunge twists* (Parivrtta Anjaneyasana), *High Crescent Lunge* (Alanasana), or any *Warrior* (Virabhadrasana) variation. From Low Lunge, students can also place their hands beside their waist on the ground or blocks or take a backbend by reaching for the floor or foot behind them.

Simplicity is also represented in common *Sun Salutation* (Surya Namaskar) asanas, such as *Chair Pose* (Utkatasana) and *forward folds,* whereby students can take time to appreciate the simple integrity of poses. Highlight that these poses are often underappreciated because they are frequently flowed through without giving proper attention to form and feeling. Have students tune into the importance of all of these simple, yet essential, elements of the poses.

More Inspiration on Simplicity

"Enjoy the little things in life because one day you'll look back and realize they were the big things." – Kurt Vonnegut

"One day I will find the right words, and they will be simple." – Jack Kerouac

"Simplicity, patience, compassion. These three are your greatest treasures. Simple in actions and thoughts, you return to the source of being. Patient with both friends and enemies, you accord with the way things are. Compassionate toward yourself, you reconcile all beings in the world." – Lao Tzu

"It's good to have money and the things that money can buy, but it's good, too, to check up once in a while and make sure that you haven't lost the things that money can't buy." – Og Mandino

"Manifest plainness,/ Embrace simplicity,/ Reduce selfishness,/ Have few desires." – Lao Tzu

"The greatest ideas are the simplest." – William Golding

"Nature is pleased with simplicity. And nature is no dummy." – Isaac Newton

- ♪ *Barely a Whisper* – Jef Martins
- ♪ *Quiet Voices* – Mike Vass
- ♪ *One River* – Benjy Wertheimer, John De Kadt

YOGA THEMES FOR MODERN YOGIS

Notes

Spaciousness

Spaciousness is to have a vast amount of room and to feel unconfined. It is about finding openness physically and psychologically in any surroundings.

Yoga allows us to practice spaciousness by demonstrating our lung capacity, identifying new ways to move, and inspiring us to set intentions to realize our potential. Thus, yoga involves making space within our body, around us, and in our everyday lives. Moreover, spaciousness is an excellent theme for modern yogis because we are often guilty of feeling confined to our circumstances despite the expansive world that surrounds us and our unlimited ability to grow.

Spaciousness as an Intention

Allow students to reflect upon how they might benefit from more spaciousness in their lives. Provide examples, such as giving oneself more time or clearing clutter. Allow this desire for spaciousness to guide their practice and inspire them to continue feeling newfound spaciousness after class. Have them dedicate their practice to finding overall spaciousness in their lives or in a particular element that comes to mind.

Centering for Spaciousness

Lead students *Matsya Mudra* (Fish Gesture), which helps to experience more spaciousness in the body by enhancing the water element within us. This aids in healing and preparing our physical bodies to gain flexibility and relaxation through asana practice, in addition to releasing dormant energy. This mudra encourages us to experience our environment as fish in open waters.

> To take this two-handed mudra, extend the index, middle, ring, and little fingers upwards while allowing the thumbs to open outwards. Place the right palm against the back of the left palm—resembling a fish and its fins.

While in Matsya Mudra, have students repeat spaciousness-inspired affirmations like the following:

> *I fill up the space around me; I allow myself to take up room; My possibilities widen every day; My mind is always expanding with knowledge and wisdom;* etc.

For more centering, guide students in meditation with closed eyes and have them imagine the space around them infinitely expanding. Meanwhile, have them fully extend their arms to eliminate any sense of confinement before taking additional movements. Allow students to marinate in the newfound space.

Students can also be led through *breath retention* (Viloma) pranayama, whereby students inhale fully and hold their breath at the top of the inhale—noticing the spaciousness of the lungs. Use this practice as a reminder to utilize the entirety of the lungs throughout the class.

Spaciousness through Asana

Have students practice a *Wide-Legged/Angle-Seated Forward Fold/Open Angle pose* (Upavistha Konasana) or *Seated Bound Angle/Butterfly Pose* (Baddha Konasana). These asanas open the hips deeply to offer spaciousness in this area of the body that can hold a significant amount of tension, yet is rarely given the opportunity to release and find space.

To find even greater spaciousness, consider leading students in a Yin Yoga sequence with longer holds. This will release deep fascial tension that interconnects throughout the body. For example, the beginning or latter part of a yoga class can include *Swan/Pigeon Pose* (Eka Pada Rajakapotasana) or a gentler *Figure-Four Stretch/Supine Pigeon* (Supta Kapotasana). These two poses create openness in the hips while releasing the fascia along the legs and spine for additional spaciousness throughout the entire body.

Furthermore, ask students to take a full-body stretch after *Corpse Pose* (Savasana). You might call this a *good morning stretch* that encourages confidence and spaciousness throughout the day.

More Inspiration in Spaciousness

"I am looking forward enormously to getting back to the sea again, where the overstimulated psyche can recover in the presence of that infinite peace and spaciousness." – C.G. Jung

"The act of meditation is being spacious." – Sogyal Rinpoche

"Above all, be at ease, be as natural and spacious as possible. Slip quietly out of the noose of your habitual anxious self, release all grasping, and relax into your true nature. Think of your ordinary emotional, thought-ridden self as a block of ice or a slab of butter left out in the sun. If you are feeling hard and cold, let this aggression melt away in the sunlight of your meditation. Let peace work on you and enable you to gather your scattered mind into the mindfulness of Calm Abiding, and awaken in you the awareness and insight of Clear Seeing. And you will find all your negativity disarmed, your aggression dissolved, and your confusion evaporating slowly like mist into the vast and stainless sky of your absolute nature." – Sogyal Rinpoche

"If you want to build a ship, don't drum up the men to gather wood, divide the work, and give orders. Instead, teach them to yearn for the vast and endless sea." – Antoine de Saint-Exupéry

- ♪ *Birth Song for Quetzalcoatl* – Xavier Quijas Yxayotl
- ♪ *Oceans of Mindfulness* – Steven Halpern
- ♪ *Opening* – Essie Jain

YOGA THEMES FOR MODERN YOGIS

Notes

III. INVIGORATION

*"If you don't like something, change it.
If you can't change it, change your attitude."*

— Maya Angelou

Yoga can help us unlock positive energy that invigorates and encourages us to take initiative towards positive change in our lives. Thus, yoga classes that surround the concept of invigoration are appropriate for modern yoga students, who can make a personal connection and find encouragement to pursue their potential.

This chapter includes five class themes to invigorate ourselves through yoga: Awakening, Creativity, Dream, Embracing Change, and Intuition.

The theme of *Awakening* helps to enliven us when our energy is more stagnant than we would like. *Creativity* as a theme encourages us to more freely and comfortably express our artistic sides. The theme of *Dream* helps us to imagine bigger dreams for ourselves and helps us to expand our understanding of what we are capable of achieving. *Embracing Change* helps us to develop skills to better adapt to life's unexpected turns and alters our routines. Last, the theme of *Intuition* helps us to recognize our gut feelings and instances when those might lead us to appropriate decision-making in a modern age.

These invigorating themes are paired with descriptions, centering exercises, asana suggestions, and inspirational material in order to connect with modern yoga students.

Awakening

Awakening is the act of becoming aware after resting or suddenly realizing greater importance in life. It involves experiencing a fresh start with clarity and positivity, and it can be felt in mind, body, and spirit.

The concept of awakening deserves to be recognized as a force throughout our yoga journeys. Awakening is fundamental to yoga because our practice prepares us for challenges to come. Yoga offers us tools to explore and be receptive to new experiences. It helps us ignite energy to achieve more with newfound energy.

An awakening-themed yoga class offers modern students an opportunity to build upon their ambitions and initiate positive change. This class intends to awaken students' yoga journeys through mental challenge and Vinyasa-inspired physical exhilaration.

Awakening as an Intention

Have students consider where they might need an encouraging nudge towards taking a new step in their lives and encourage them to dedicate this practice to themselves. This could be something we have not started yet and would like to initiate, or have put off and would like to revisit. Assure them that everything that exists has begun somewhere, and have them ignite their inner potential through this practice. Thus, encourage students to set an intention surrounding how they can initiate a personal awakening.

Centering for Awakening

Practice Uttarabodhi Mudra I (Supreme Awakening Gesture), which helps to tap into the source of one's inspiration, creates new energy and calms the nervous system.

To take this mudra, clasp the hands with the palms facing downwards, extend the index fingers upwards and extend the thumbs downwards to form a diamond-like shape.

Having students hold the mudra, ask them to repeat affirmations such as the following:

I am healthy; I am happy; I am full of energy; I live a life of opportunity and abundance; I experience new awakenings each day; etc.

To continue centering, lead students in a meditation that encourages students to look inward and recognize the potential that they hope to awaken during the practice. Keeping their intention in mind, have students imagine a tangible flame within their body and tap into feelings of determination and self-encouragement that make their flame burn brighter. Encourage students to keep this fiery feeling alive during their practice.

Furthermore, review *Ujjayi* Pranayama, or victorious breath, to ignite inner energy that will guide students throughout the practice. Have students inhale positive energy and exhale stagnant matter.

Awakening Through Asana

Fire Toes Pose/Toe Squat awakens the fascia along the tissues of the feet and spine through a fiery stretch and encourages overall flexibility. This asana can be taken with both feet while sitting onto the heels, or with one foot while the other foot is propped off the floor in a figure-four quad stretch.

Another way to experience a sense of awakening is by taking *Lion Pose* (Simhasana) & practicing *Lion's Breath* (Simhasana Pranayama), which energizes the body as if it were a lion that is ready to lunge.

Locust Pose (Salabhasana) also awakens the core by requiring muscle activation and stretching from head to toe—allowing the entire body to feel filled with life.

Bound Angle/Butterfly Pose (Baddha Konasana) also represents the concept of awakening by signifying the transformation from a cocoon into a butterfly. The pose also offers a hip stretch that relieves tension and awakens the body for additional external hip openers. Bound Angle can also be taken with a forward bend to deepen the stretch and sense of awakening. Cue students to continue lengthening and awakening their entire spines.

More Inspiration on Awakening

"And the day came when the risk to remain tight in a bud was more painful than the risk it took to blossom." – Anaïs Nin -

"You don't need to earn your awakening, you just need to put both feet in and remember to wake up. Now. And now. And now." – Jessica Graham

"You don't have to be great to start, / but you have to start to be great." – Zig Ziglar

"A year from now you may wish you had started today." – Karen Lamb

"Start where you are. Use what you have. Do what you can." – Arthur Ashe

- ♪ *Awakening Now* – Sambodhi Prem
- ♪ *Awake* – Lambert
- ♪ *Countdown* – Sarah Watson

Notes

Creativity

Creativity is the ability to produce something new, original, or imaginative. Creativity requires self-expression and allows one to channel their energy into something that honors themselves. With courage and risk, creativity becomes art.

Creativity relates to the yogic principle of *Brahmacharya*, which is characterized as abstinence to be closer to the divine. By practicing Brahmacharya, our sexual energy can be channeled through creativity, allowing us to heighten our creative abilities.

To channel creativity in a Western and contemporary yoga practice, we can focus on utilizing a more efficient use of energy and allowing ourselves to apply more of our energy toward nourishing our creative and artistic sides.

Creativity as an Intention

Explain to students that if we have an event-filled day or week, an exhausting and frustrating experience, or distractions while doing tasks that do not deserve the amount of attention that they are receiving, we neglect time for creative expression. Thus, we must learn to recognize when we are pushing ourselves too far or spending too much time on something that consumes our energy. In this regard, encourage students to set practice intentions surrounding the concept of energy conservation so that they can better prioritize and let their unique creative energy flourish.

Centering for Creativity

Take *Matangi Mudra* (Guardian of Wisdom Gesture), which helps to connect us to our creative energy and overall harmony with the world around us. This mudra is appropriately named after the goddess Matangi—the guardian of the arts, who inspires creativity and freedom of expression.

To take this mudra, clasp both hands together with the left thumb crossed over the right thumb, and extend the middle fingers upwards together.

While maintaining Matangi Mudra, have students repeat creativity-inspiring affirmations, such as the following:

I am a creative soul; I nourish my creativity; I channel my energy efficiently; I express my true self; etc.

Furthermore, lead students in *Nadi Shodhana* Pranayama with retention—holding in and releasing creative energy while playing with their breath in a playful way. After guiding students through a few rounds, have students repeat several rounds in their own time to tune into the flow of their unique energy and creative mindset.

Creativity through Asanas

Creativity can be ignited and cultivated through asana practice that works on energy conservation and incorporates creative movement.

For example, *Fallen Triangle/Star* (Patita Tarasana), *Wild Thing* (Camatkarasana), and *Side Lunge Pose* (Skandasana) represent creativity because they all require deliberate strength-based holds, creative flexibility, and an open heart and mind. These beautiful poses require significant muscle engagement with mental ease, and they energize us for other asanas throughout the practice. Give students time to play in these poses while moving intuitively and with creativity.

Fallen Triangle offers different shoulder stretch variations that students can try by gracefully repositioning their raised arm—such as reaching it over their head or allowing it to extend at an angle. Students can also try bending the knees or lifting the hips higher. In Wild Thing, students can decide whether to straighten one or both legs or reach the raised arm over their head. Furthermore, Side Lunge offers numerous arm variations and opportunities to move intuitively and creatively into the hips. For example,

students can keep their hands in a prayer position, touch the floor, sit on a block, or shift from side to side in a dynamic stretch. Allow students to play, try something new, and express themselves.

Additional Inspiration for Creativity

"Creativity is a combination of discipline and a childlike spirit." – Robert Greene

"To be creative means to be in love with life. You can be creative only if you love life enough that you want to enhance its beauty, you want to bring a little more music to it, a little more poetry to it, a little more dance to it." – Osho

"Creativity is intelligence having fun." – Albert Einstein

"Life isn't about finding yourself. Life is about creating yourself." – George Bernard Shaw

"Don't let your special character and values, the secret that you know and no one else does, the truth – don't let that get swallowed up by the great chewing complacency." – Aesop

"The mind is for having ideas, not for holding them." – David Allen

"Instead of worrying about what you cannot control, shift your energy to what you can create." – Roy T. Bennett

"I have learnt through bitter experience the one supreme lesson to conserve my anger, and as heat conserved is transmuted into energy, even so our anger controlled can be transmuted into a power which can move the world." – Mahatma Gandhi

- ♪ *Snow* – Sarah Watson
- ♪ *Dancing Clouds* – Kristoffer Walin, Ora W Jansson
- ♪ *Midnight Sky* – Petit Biscuit

YOGA THEMES FOR MODERN YOGIS

Notes

Dream

Dreaming is the first step towards creating a goal in our minds. Dreaming allows us to visualize our ideal future, and it allows us to mimic positive emotions that we might experience if those dreams come true. While dreams can have a negative connotation when they are considered synonymous with unrealistic aspirations, dreams help us foresee our goals before they materialize, and they help guide our path in a positive direction.

Dreaming is an appropriate modern yoga class theme because it is simple to conceptualize. We all have aspirations, and yoga can help us enter the mindset that ongoing effort allows us to achieve goals and dreams. Yoga represents how dreams should be supported by practice so that they can materialize.

Dream as an Intention

Give students a moment to consider some of their dreams. While these can be their wildest fantasies, encourage them to think of a dream that is within their power to make a reality. Have them narrow that down to one big dream, and have them set that as their practice intention to find mental clarity to pursue it. Let that dream guide them to invigorate themselves throughout class to help make it come true off of the mat.

Centering to Dream

Have students take Kubera Mudra II (Guardian of Wealth Gesture), which helps to concentrate energy that can be directed toward achieving goals and dreams. It is said to also clarify one's envisioned path, encourage virtuous desires, and bring about courage in order to succeed.

> To take this mudra, pinch the thumb, index, and middle fingers together, while drawing the pinky and ring fingers into the palm. The palm faces upwards.

Holding the mudra for additional concentration, ask students to repeat dream-inspiring affirmations like the following:

I allow myself to dream; I can make my dreams a reality; my dreams are attainable; I trust myself to follow my dreams; My dreams are more than fantasies; etc.

Furthermore, have students close their eyes and encourage their breathing to become heavier, longer, and more relaxed— as If they are entering a dreamy sleep-like state. Then, lead students in a *day trip* meditation and allow their minds to take them anywhere and let them do anything on that trip for a few moments. Simply, allow them to indulge in a daydream and feel at ease. After a minute, guide their attention toward their practice intention and have them imagine how it feels to have a daydream become reality. Encourage students to revisit that rewarding feeling throughout class.

Dream Through Asana

A dream-like mindset can be nourished through challenging arm balances, including *Crow/Crane Pose* (Bakasana), *Peacock Pose* (Mayurasana), and *Firefly Pose* (Tittibhasana) among others. These winged animal-inspired poses represent our ability to fly beyond everyday expectations and challenge ourselves to see from a new perspective.

Another simple and symbolic movement is raising our hands high to the sky, stretching out in an *Upward Salute* (Urdhva Hastasana) or *Chair Pose* (Utkatasana) while gazing upwards— embracing an unrestrained feeling of possibility and our power to dream.

Another option is to practice Yoga Nidra techniques, whereby students can enter *Corpse Pose* (Savasana) for an extended period of time while being led in a guided meditation. This style of practice helps students enter a dream-like state. Yoga Nidra can also help students connect the concepts of dreaming and reality.

More Dream Inspiration

"You are never too old to set another goal / or to dream a new dream." – C.S. Lewis

"The future belongs to those who believe in the beauty of their dreams." – Eleanor Roosevelt

"Be clearly aware of the stars and infinity on high. Then life seems almost enchanted after all." – Vincent Van Gogh

"Nurture your mind with great thoughts, for you will never go any higher than you think." – Benjamin Disraeli

"Anything you can imagine, you can create." – Oprah Winfrey

"Worry is the misuse of the imagination." – Dan Zandra

"Those who dream by day are cognizant of many things which escape those who dream only by night." – Edgar Allan Poe

- ♪ *Dream 13 (minus even)* – Max Richter, Clarice Jensen, Ben Russel
- ♪ *Dreams are Real* – No Spirit, Kyle McEvoy
- ♪ *Oceansize* – Oh Wonder
- ♪ *Dream A Little Dream of Me* – The Mamas & The Papas

Notes

Embracing Change

Constant change is inevitable as the world and our circumstances evolve every day— such as our environment, physical characteristics, finances, relationships, and emotions. Even if we resist change, countless elements of our lives become different as we age. Unexpected opportunities, dangers, and natural phenomena also occur that are out of our control. However, we are in control of how we react to changes. If they are welcomed and understood, we can mitigate change-induced stress and be equipped to adapt with optimism. And to strengthen these skills, we can incorporate the concept of embracing change into our yoga practice.

Yoga represents a positive outlook on change because the more consistent our practice, the easier it becomes and the more opportunities we will have to challenge ourselves. Still, we must accept that our bodies feel different every day and not every pose will be accessible. The secret is to be kind and understanding of ourselves. By practicing this mantra, we can encourage ourselves to also be kind and understanding when changes occur in our modern everyday lives.

Embracing Change as an Intention

Have students consider how any circumstances in their life have recently changed. Provide general examples, such as work, routine, family, social life, or health. Then, allow students to form an intention about embracing change in their life, rather than fighting against it. Allow them to consider how that gives them a sense of relief.

Centering for Embracing Change

Take *Shakti Mudra* (Essence of Power & Creative Force Gesture), which connects us to our supportive energy and encourages us to be adaptive to change.

To create this two-handed mudra, make fists with the thumb tucked inside each hand and bring the outside of the fingers of both hands together. Then, connect the tips of the ring fingers and the tips of the pinky fingers.

You might also incorporate affirmations for embracing change, such as these:

I enjoy all the twists and turns of life; I am understanding of changes; I adapt to change with ease; etc.

Further, have students reflect on how they are feeling before guiding them through breathwork. Have them inhale the future and exhale the past. After several rounds, have students consider any changes in their body and mind from when the exercise began.

If other pranayama exercises are incorporated, have students consider how these breathing exercises also bring positive change into their lives. For example, simply lengthening the count of exhales can help relax the body and enter a clearer and calmer state of mind that is more accepting of changing circumstances.

Embracing Change Through Asanas

Inversions represent changes in body orientation and perspective when the feet are raised above the head and heart. Examples of inversion poses that help us to appreciate change include variations of *Headstand* (Sirsasana), *Candlestick* (Supta Dandasana), and Plow Pose (Halasana). More advanced students can try *Handstand* (Adho Mukha Vrksasana) or *Scorpion Pose* (Vrischikasana).

These asanas might sound daunting or uncomfortable, but once students attempt inversions, they can appreciate the beauty and benefits of change and a fresh perspective—feeling changes in blood circulation and their point of view. Allow students to stay in these positions for at least ten breaths at a time to allow time to contemplate their change in orientation.

More Inspiration for Embracing Change

"We delight in the beauty of the butterfly, but rarely admit the changes it has gone through to achieve that beauty." – Maya Angelou

"The measure of intelligence is the ability to change." – Albert Einstein

"Intelligence is the ability to adapt to change." – Stephen Hawking

"By changing nothing, nothing happens." – Tony Robbins

"If you're brave enough to say goodbye, life will reward you with a new hello." – Paulo Coelho

"I cannot say whether things will get better if we change; what I can say is they must change if they are to get better." – Georg Christoph Lichtenberg

"The secret of change is to focus all of your energy not on fighting the old, but on building the new." – Socrates

"Nothing is absolute. Everything changes." – Frida Kahlo

"We must be willing to let go of the life we planned so as to have the life that is waiting for us." – Joseph Campbell

"Life is like riding a bicycle. To keep your balance, you have to keep moving." – Albert Einstein

- ♪ *Unstoppable Changes* – Sebastian Zawadzki
- ♪ *Chattr Chattr Vartee* – Nirinjan Kaur, Matthew Schoening
- ♪ *Landslide* – Fleetwood Mac

INVIGORATION

Notes

Intuition

Intuition is the ability to gain insight through thought and inference while allowing us to quickly come to conclusions. In many cases, we need evidence to support conclusions, but as humans, we sometimes like to over-rationalize and overthink decisions that should come from our gut instinct.

Intuition is an important yoga class theme for modern yogis because it can help to guide us in making decisions that are best for us and looking within ourselves for answers. This is represented by a practice that encourages intuitive movement and breath that inspires us to follow our hearts.

Intuition as an Intention

Explain to students that we have all been in circumstances where we wished we had listened to ourselves and followed our gut instinct. These situations exemplify how we are often our best guide and that important and life-shaping decisions should be influenced by our intuition. As such, encourage students to set an intention surrounding how they might wish to trust their intuition going forward.

Centering with Intuition

Take *Shankha Varta Mudra* (Conch Livelihood mudra) which is said to draw the attention inward and provide clarity and insight, thereby enhancing intuition and allowing us to listen to our inner voice.

> To take this two-handed mudra, make a diamond shape with both hands—touching the thumbs together and pointing them towards the ground, and touching the other fingers together towards the sky. Then, draw the right index finger down to make a suspended half-of-a-heart shape on the right side.

Have students take intuition-inspiring affirmations, such as the following:

> *I know myself more than anyone; trust my intuition; I am headed in the right direction; I am my best guide*; etc.

Moreover, guide students in taking a few breaths together before asking them to breathe intuitively. For example, ask them whether their bodies are asking for longer or deeper breaths, longer exhales than inhales, retention between breaths, or a greater expansion of the belly. Encourage students to take what they intuitively need to feel more comfortable and centered.

Intuition Through Asana

Let students listen to their bodies and express how they feel through intuitive movement. This style of practice can be articulated in *Cat and Cow Tilts* (Chakravakasana), as well as *Downward-Facing Dog* (Adho Mukha Svanasana)—both of which can involve intuitive movement, controlled stretches, and several options that you might propose.

Suggestions can include walking out the dog and taking *Downward-Facing Dog* (Adho Mukha Svanasana) twists. Students can also try leaning forward and back when taking Cat and Cow hip tilts. Pausing in a neutral *Tabletop Pose* (Bharmanasana), have students intuitively draw a shoulder and hip towards one another in a C-shape and repeat this on each side. If students desire more spinal movements, have them take a *Naughty Kitten* by having them circle their hips while taking any Tabletop movements mentioned here.

Also, remind students to use their intuitive discretion throughout the class, especially when challenging themselves or paying attention to how their bodies are feeling on a particular day. These are reminders to practice applying our intuition throughout our daily lives.

More Inspiration on Intuition

"Let yourself be silently drawn by the strange pull of what you really love. It will not lead you astray." – Rumi

"At various points in our lives, or on a quest, and for reasons that often remain obscure, we are driven to make decisions which prove with hindsight to be loaded with meaning." – Swami Satchidananda

"Intuition is seeing with the soul." – Dean Koontz

"Have the courage to follow your heart and intuition. They somehow already know what you truly want to become. Everything else is secondary." – Steve Jobs

"The only real valuable thing is intuition." – Albert Einstein

- ♪ *Catskill* – Kyle McEvoy
- ♪ *Nectar Drop* – DJ Drez
- ♪ *Float* – Sol Rising
- ♪ *Who Says* – John Mayer

Notes

IV. EMPOWERMENT

"The best way to predict your future is to create it"

— Abraham Lincoln

Empowerment means granting one's self power to achieve tasks and goals. Thus, empowerment is necessary every day in order to grow, progress, and thrive.

The previous chapter of this book includes modern yoga themes relating to how we can invigorate ourselves through yoga. This chapter builds upon that overarching theme by introducing eight yoga class themes for encouraging ourselves to act upon our aspirations and take the required steps to be the best versions of ourselves. These practice themes underscore how yoga can inspire us to find empowerment within. These themes are Courage, Expansiveness, Healing, Inner-Flame, Patience, Perseverance, Reassurance, and Self-Confidence.

The theme of *Courage* ignites inner bravery to take initial steps towards achieving something without knowing whether success will result. *Expansiveness* as a theme encourages us to take up more space both physically and figuratively to feel a sense of spaciousness. *Healing* helps us to use yoga as an instrument for overcoming obstacles. The theme of *Inner-Flame* helps us to fuel our inner ambitions so that they can be put into practice. *Patience* encourages us to accept the process of waiting despite the inconvenience. *Perseverance* as a class theme inspires the motivation to overcome difficulties and better ourselves. Next, the theme of *Reassurance* offers comfort when we might appreciate the encouragement. Last, a *Self-Confidence* themed class helps us to believe in ourselves and our decisions.

These themes surrounding empowerment are discussed with reference to their overall significance to modern yogis—drawing connections through mindfulness techniques, asanas, and inspirational material.

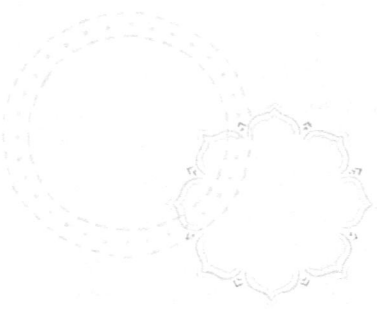

Courage

Courage involves inner strength that allows us to persevere and it is the first step towards empowering ourselves. Courage requires bravery, confidence, and self-encouragement—which can be easier said than done. Yet, yoga can help us achieve these qualities and allow us to be more courageous in our modern day-to-day lives.

The way we understand and employ courage looks different for everyone and is relative to our changing circumstances. In yoga, sometimes courage is about committing to a shape or challenging ourselves; Other times, courage is about accepting and celebrating where we are today and not worrying about how we look.

Courage as an Intention

Have students consider how courage looks different to us throughout our daily lives and our yoga practice. For example, courage can look different depending on what we are doing—whether that is trying something new, stepping outside of our comfort zone, or taking risks. Allow students to then consider a specific way that additional courage might help them succeed—whether that relates to yoga or any element or elements of their life.

Encourage students to set an intention surrounding how they can embrace courageousness, however that might apply to them. Then, ask students to have the courage to let go of everything that no longer serves them.

Centering with Courage

Take *Kali Mudra* (Black Goddess Gesture), which increases energy and taps into our inner courage and strength.

To practice this mudra, clasp both hands together while extending the ring fingers together as they touch at the finger pads, and straighten the crossed pinky fingers with the right pinky finger on the outside.

As another centering technique, have students repeat courage-themed affirmations such as the following:

I am brave; I am courageous like a lion; I believe in every leap that I take; I embrace my inner strength; I am confident and empowered; etc.

Furthermore, have students tap into their inner courage by inhaling feelings of bravery and exhaling doubts and fears. Have them repeat this several times while keeping their practice intentions in mind. After, have students pause and feel a greater sense of courageousness.

Courage through Asana

Have students work towards *the Splits* (Hanumanasana), which is named after the Hindu god Hanuman who took a giant leap of faith that no one else had succeeded in taking. By doing so, Hanuman lifted a curse and saved a life. The story behind this asana's name represents how courage can lead to positive change. The Splits also have variations if students wish to try something new, such as reaching their arms up or reaching back to grab the back foot. Students can also put a slight bend in both knees to make a zig-zag shape across the legs. Simpler variations include taking half-splits or sliding the hips down with blocks on each side of the body to elevate the hands and keep the hips higher off of the ground.

Hero Pose (Virasana) also represents courage because it involves sitting on the shins in a proud and confident fashion. Hero Pose, like the Splits, also offers students room to work towards deeper variations with the chest and the crown of the head held high. In this case, *Reclined Hero Pose* (Supta Virasana) can be achieved by slowly walking the hands back until students can lay on the ground behind them. The full pose can be taken with a bolster or blankets to support the back and relax deeper into the pose.

More Inspiration on Courage

"If it scares you, it might be a good thing to try." — Seth Godin

"Don't be afraid to give up the good to go for the great." — John D. Rockefeller

"Success is not final, failure is not fatal: it is the courage to continue that counts." — Winston Churchill

"Most of the shadows in life are caused by standing in our own sunshine." — Ralph Waldo Emerson

"Indecision steals many years from many people who wind up wishing they'd just had the courage to leap." — Doe Zantamata

"You can never leave footprints that last if you are always walking on tiptoe." — Leymah Gbowee

"I am convinced that courage is the most important of all the virtues. Because without courage, you cannot practice any other virtue consistently. You can be kind for a while; you can be generous for a while; you can be just for a while, or merciful for a while, even loving for a while. But it is only with courage that you can be persistently and insistently kind and generous and fair." — Maya Angelou

"One day you will wake up and there won't be any more time to do all the things you've always wanted to do. Do them now." — Paulo Coelho

- ♪ *Aap Sahaee Hoa* (Krishan Liquid Mix) — Krishan, Jai-Jaddeesh
- ♪ *Tongue* — Edamame
- ♪ *I See Fire* — Jasmine Thompson

YOGA THEMES FOR MODERN YOGIS

Notes

Expansiveness

To expand means to become fuller, take up more space, and gradually work towards capacity. It can also mean to become more extensive by building upon something to make it greater, more developed, or more substantial.

Through yoga, we can explore the concept of expansiveness by training ourselves to take up additional space in our own means—physically and emotionally through deep heart, throat, and shoulder opening positions. These expansive-inspired elements in yoga practice also help to open the throat and heart chakras that help us become more loving and to be more inclined to speak the truth.

Expansiveness as an Intention

Explain to students that in a bustling, growing, demanding, increasingly digital, and modern world, we can begin to feel small and confined. This mindset can prevent us from feeling fully in charge of our lives and we can forget that we always have the ability to adapt by taking up more space and expanding our minds. Examples of how to do this include going for a nature walk or practicing expansiveness-themed yoga techniques—such as those incorporated in this class.

Encourage students' intentions to surround expansiveness where they need it most, or to generally make more space and open up in various ways. Mention that expansiveness begins within ourselves—which this class focuses on.

Expansiveness through Mindfulness

Take *Vistara Mudra* (Expansiveness Gesture), which increases sensitivity to energy in a powerful way. It is also said to improve the body's blood circulation and encourage its self-healing capacity.

To take this two-handed mudra, extend the forearms away from the body and in line with the belly. Close any gaps between the five fingers on each hand and face the palms towards one another while keeping roughly ten inches between them—representing an expanded space between both hands.

Consider having students repeat affirmations, such as the following:

I make space for positivity; I open myself to the world around me; I have infinite room to expand; I allow myself to take up more space; My heart and mind expand; etc.

For a pranayama practice, focus on fully expanding the lungs. Have students place one hand on the belly as they breathe. Feel the belly rise with each inhale, and fall with each exhale. Meanwhile, have students imagine the lungs filling up as the diaphragm lowers, and the air release as the diaphragm rises and the belly button draws inward. Have them notice that with deeper inhales and greater lung expansion, they will feel more energized and experience an overall sense of expansiveness.

Expansiveness through Asana

To experience expansiveness through poses, focus on *Extended Triangle Pose* (Utthita Trikonasana) and its variations, such *as Twisted/Revolved Triangle* (Parivrtta Trikonasana). Students can take Triangle Pose with a block to focus on the integrity and heart-opening nature of the pose.

You might also begin with *Lunge Twist* (Parivrtta Anjaneyasana) openings and reaching an arm to the sky in *Tabletop Pose* (Bharmanasana) to practice before straightening the front leg. These poses encourage a sense of physical and emotional expansiveness by opening the chest, arms, and hips.

Making sure to demonstrate appropriate backbend preparation, you might also integrate poses that release the throat, chest, shoulders to feel an expansiveness in various parts of the body at once. For example, a pose that incorporates all of these elements at once is *Camel Pose* (Ustrasana). Camel opens and physically expands the chest, throat, shoulders, and hips while releasing stress and negative emotion that allows us to find greater expansion within.

More Inspiration on Expansiveness

"Do not feel lonely, the entire universe is inside you. Stop acting so small. You are the universe in ecstatic motion. Set your life on fire. Seek those who fan your flames." — Rumi

"Most people overestimate what they can do in one year and underestimate what they can do in ten years." — Bill Gates

"When one door of happiness closes, another opens; but often we look so long at the closed door that we do not see the one which has been opened for us." — Helen Keller

"I remembered that the real world was wide, and that a varied field of hopes and fears, of sensations and excitements, awaited those who had the courage to go forth into its expanse, to seek real knowledge of life amidst its perils." — Charlotte Brontë

"Your hand opens and closes, opens and closes. If it were always a fist or always stretched open, you would be paralyzed. Your deepest presence is in every small contracting and expanding, the two as beautifully balanced and coordinated as birds' wings." — Rumi

- ♪ *The Golden Path* — Kumbhaka
- ♪ *Beginnings* — MC YOGI, East Forest
- ♪ *Explorers of Infinity* — Marti Nikko, DJ Drez, Eddie Young
- ♪ *Into the Mystic* — Van Morrison

YOGA THEMES FOR MODERN YOGIS

Notes

Healing

Healing means to overcome hardship, pain, or adversity. It is a difficult process that can require patience and time in order to move forward, continue onward, and forgive. Healing cannot erase the past, but it helps us feel better and be better equipped to approach future endeavors with greater clarity and positivity.

Yoga can help us to experience healing both psychologically and physically. Our physical bodies can heal by moving in ways that agree with us. Healing through yoga can also involve a long-term commitment to improving health, strength, and flexibility, which helps us to feel our best and prevent injury. Furthermore, yoga heals us psychologically by helping us discover mindfulness and overcome emotional difficulties. Moreover, yoga helps us to enter a mindset that is more conducive to overcoming adversity.

Healing as an Intention

Allow students to consider any part of their life that requires healing in order for them to live a healthier and more positive life. For example, this might relate to something that has weighed on them for a while, a recent loss or accident, or anything that has recently left them feeling disappointed. Have students surround their intention around this theme of healing before practicing exercises that encourage us to heal on and off of the mat.

Healing through Mindfulness

While all mudras are said to heal our bodies in some way, lead students into *Pitta Energizing Mudra* (Blues-Banishing Gesture), which helps to reignite our healing energy. It helps us to have a more positive outlook, encourage self-esteem, and overcome depression that might hold us back.

> This mudra involves both hands. With the right hand, place the tip of the thumb on the right side of the ring finger and press the index finger on the thumb—just

above the first joint. With the left hand, touch the tips of the thumb and pinky finger together.

Maintaining the mudra, have students take affirmations for healing such as the following:

I heal every day; healing is a process, no matter how small; Time will heal everything; everything will get better; I allow myself to heal; etc.

As a Pranayama practice, have students locate where they might be feeling physical or emotional discomfort and have them breathe into that sensation. You can suggest breathing in healing energy, and exhaling discomfort or pain. This breathing exercise can be revisited during asana practice during holds and stretches.

Healing through Asanas

Restorative yoga positions are beneficial for healing both physically and emotionally. For example, consider guiding students into a simple *Legs Up-The-Wall Pose* (Viparita Karani) and offer the option of sliding their mat up to a wall or placing a prop under their seat to fully rest and restore in the position that suits them.

Another recovery position is *Child's Pose* (Balasana) that feels especially restorative when taken with the arms close to the body and the palms facing upwards to receive healing energy.

Students will also experience healing in *Corpse Pose* (Savasana) by allowing their bodies to come to complete stillness. This is the only way for our bodies to truly heal and take in the full benefits of the practice.

More Inspiration on Healing

"It is being honest about my pain that makes me invincible." — Nayyirah Waheed

EMPOWERMENT

"The highest reward for a person's toil is not what they get for it, but what they become by it." – John Ruskin

"The way I see it, if you want the rainbow, you gotta put up with the rain." – Dolly Parton

"I wish I could tell you it gets better, but it doesn't get better. You get better." – Joan Rivers

"The flower that blooms in adversity is the rarest and most beautiful of all." – Walt Disney Company (Mulan)

"One day, in retrospect, the years of struggle will strike you as the most beautiful." – Sigmund Freud

- ♪ *Healing Shores* – Ty Burhoe, Bill Douglas
- ♪ *Hands* – Jewel
- ♪ *Healing the Heart* – Parijat
- ♪ *Heal Me* – Nirinjan Kaur

Notes

Inner-Flame

Our inner-flame is a deeply-rooted desire within us to achieve our passions. It is fueled by self-discipline and is about working towards something repeatedly, even when that venture is not easy.

The concept of an inner-flame also relates to the yogic concept of *Tapas*, which translates from Sanskrit to fire or to burn. Thus, an inner-flame themed class helps to bring traditional yoga philosophy into a modern light.

Yoga itself represents an internal flame that requires discipline to safely progress. While some yoga techniques have immediate benefits, other techniques and asanas require practice. Accepting this can help to avoid frustration and help to inspire us to continue towards a goal. We can revisit the mat and improve our practice while also becoming more passionate and curious. Thus, a yoga theme surrounding an internal flame can inspire us to persevere and nurture our ambitions.

Inner-Flame as an Intention

Allow students' intentions to surround an inner fire that exists within them. As encouragement, ask them what they want to burn brighter. Ask what they are willing to work hard for, or what they would like to dedicate themselves to. You might give examples of something personal to them, such as a long-term goal, an endeavor they have put aside, or a passion project that they would like to revisit and improve upon. Have them select something that stands out to them and let that flame and overall mentality fuel their practice.

Inner-Flame Mindfulness

Lead students into *Surya Mudra* (Sun Seal Gesture), which kindles inspiration, fuels energy and cleanses the body of impurities that might stand in the way of connecting to an inner flame.

> To take this mudra, hold down the ring finger with the thumb and rest the hand on the thigh while keeping the palm facing up.

While holding Surya Mudra, have students repeat affirmations such as the following:

> *I kindle my inner flame; the light in me shines bright; I illuminate my surroundings; I let my dreams flourish*; etc.

Pairing meditation with pranayama, have students breathe cool air up a lengthened spine, close their eyes and release their shoulders on their exhales, while noticing the warmth of their natural breath and a continuous inner-heat. Meanwhile, have students notice the colors in a flame through closed eyelids.

Further, you might incorporate *Kapalabhati* pranayama (skull cleansing breath) to help fuel the inner fire energy, and towards the end of practice, you might lead students in *Sitali* pranayama (cooling breath) to help lower the body temperature after a fiery practice.

Inner-Flame Asanas

Dedicate time for core work that fires and awakens and warms up the body. These will boost confidence and prepare for a faster-paced flow with a challenging peak asana. Core work can include a balancing *Tabletop Pose* (Bharmanasana) with opposite arm and leg reaches. After extending both limbs, have students draw the lifted opposite knee and elbow towards one another in a crunch. Repeating this several times on each side will ignite the inner-flame within the body's core. Students can also

challenge themselves to balance on one knee in a Tabletop position while touching the lifted knee to the toes of the grounded leg.

Fiery crunches can also be taken from *Downward-Facing Dog* (Adho Mukha Svanasana), which offers a more challenging variation of Tabletop crunches with an additional range of motion.

Some additional fiery asanas that can be incorporated as peak poses include holding *Chair Pose* (Utkatasana) variations, *Boat Pose* (Navasana), or *Low Plank* (Chaturanga) push-ups. Let burning sensations during difficult poses remind students that strength and reward take hard work and dedication.

More Inner-Flame Inspiration

"I am not afraid of failing / I'm afraid my potential / might set the world on fire" — Rupi Kaur

"The practice must be steady, continuous, and over a period of time." — Patañjali

"It is not because things are difficult that we do not dare, it is because we do not dare that they are difficult." — Seneca

"The light burning within you is a far more accurate reflection of who you are than the stories you've been telling yourself." — Grace Bullock

"there are days / when the light flickers / and then I remember / I am the light / I go in and / switch it back on" — Rupi Kaur

- ♪ *I Need a Forest Fire* — James Blake, Bon Iver
- ♪ *Soon it Will Be Cold Enough to Build Fires* — Emancipator
- ♪ *Alive* — Ouska

EMPOWERMENT

Notes

Patience

Patience is the ability to wait despite inconvenience and difficulty. It also challenges us to avoid feeling impatient and annoyed when delays interrupt our plans or exceed our expectations.

Patience is a virtuous quality because it allows us to feel at ease no matter how long we must await or postpone something. This could relate to a goal or waiting on something that is out of our control. We must also be patient with others when they compromise a planned schedule.

In yoga, we cannot force ourselves into positions and have no choice but to be patient and practice so that we do not hurt ourselves attempting something that we are not prepared for. Thus, by practicing patience on the mat, we can also strengthen our ability to be patient in everyday circumstances.

Patience as an Intention

Allow students to consider a recent instant when they have been inpatient and how that has only made matters worse. Examples might include waiting in line, waiting for a response, waiting to meet someone, or waiting for something to arrive. Have students set an intention relating to something that they are waiting for, reminding them of the power of their minds and assuring them that they have the patience to wait.

Patience Through Mindfulness

Have students take *Tambula/Ardha Suchi Mudra* (Sprout Gesture), which represents a sprouting flower or plant and can be interpreted as how everything starts small and takes time to grow.

To practice this mudra, raise the index finger as if to point at something in the sky. Keep the thumb parallel to the index finger and the other fingers tucked into the palm.

While holding the mudra, ask students to repeat affirmations relating to patience, such as the following:

Good things always come to me if I show patience; The best things take time; I have patience for myself and others; I release tension by practicing patience; etc.

Furthermore, guide students in a *box breathing* pranayama exercise that helps to occupy and calm the mind. This is a type of breath retention (Viloma) exercise that involves breathing in, pausing, breathing out, pausing, and repeating this four-step pattern. For box breathing, each breath and pause are held for the same count of four—the number of corners in a square box. This exercise gives the mind something to focus on while calming the parasympathetic nervous system that regulates stress, mood, and other involuntary functions that are challenged by impatience.

Patience Through Asana

Patience is represented through *King Dancer Pose* (Natarajasana), which can require years of progression to reach the full expression and flipped hand grip. Students might begin learning this balancing and hip and chest opening pose with a strap before opening the shoulders enough to eventually reach the arms overhead to grab the lifted back foot.

Patience can also be practiced by working towards full *Wheel/Upward Bow Pose* (Urdhva Dhanurasana) and its variations, including lifting one leg to the sky or straightening both legs. Another asana that represents patience is *Frog Pose* (Mandukasana), where students can release lower to the ground throughout their yoga journeys and eventually reach *Center/Straddle Splits Pose* (Samakonasana).

Additionally, patience is represented by any pose that students are working towards in a class or through a series of classes. With each step toward reaching a pose, highlight students' progression and note their achievements as examples of patience and its rewards.

More Inspiration on Patience

"If you are that patient, your mind is more settled, and what you do will be more perfect. If you are unsettled and anxious to get the result... nothing done with that disturbed mind will have quality. So, it is not only how long you practice, but with what patience, what earnestness and what quality..." – Swami Satchidananda

"Be not afraid of growing slowly; be afraid only of growing still." – Chinese Proverb

"Anything worth having is worth waiting for." – Susan Elizabeth Philips

"Don't judge each day by the harvest you reap but by the seeds you plant." – Robert Lewis Stevenson

"The man who moves mountains begins by carrying small stones." – Confucius

"It is better to take many small stones in the right direction than to make a great leap forward only to stumble backwards. – Chinese proverb

"Accept the pace of nature. Her secret is patience." – Ralph Waldo Emerson

"The slow way is the fast way." – Zen Proverb

"Patience is not the ability to wait, but how you act while you're waiting." – Joyce Meyer

"When we develop patience, we find that we develop a reserve of calm and tranquility." – Dalai Lama

- ♪ *Patience* – The Lumineers
- ♪ *Patience* – Rhye, Ólafur Arnalds
- ♪ *Dreamcatcher* – Kamal

EMPOWERMENT

Notes

Perseverance

Perseverance means to practice persistence towards achieving a goal irrespective of difficulties and delays. Thus, perseverance requires inner drive, self-encouragement, determination, dedication, and resilience. Luckily, these are qualities that can be nourished through yoga practice

Perseverance requires patience with the added elements of active effort and self-motivation. Yoga can help us to achieve this through repetition to build physical and mental stamina that can help us to achieve goals on and off of the mat.

Perseverance as an Intention

Have students consider something that they are working towards that has been taking a while. This could be something that has taken much longer than they had anticipated or something more difficult than they had imagined. This endeavor should also be something that they are still willing to keep working towards. For example, this could relate to their health, career, family, or something else important to them.

Have students dedicate this class towards fueling their inner perseverance so that they are inspired to keep working towards their ambitions.

Perseverance Centering

Take *Abhaya Hrdaya Mudra* (Fearless Heart Gesture), which helps to conduct energy, create vitality, assist in healing, and bring calmness. These qualities help to persevere through challenges.

> To create this two-handed mudra, pinch the thumb and ring fingers together on each hand and bring the backsides of the palms together. Hook together both pinky fingers, both middle fingers, and both index fingers together.

Have students repeat the following, or similar affirmations related to perseverance:

> *I am shaped by my perseverance; With hard work and practice, I will succeed; my resilience shapes my character; I am strong and steadfast; I will not stray from my path*; etc.

Furthermore, review *Ujjayi* Pranayama with students and reinforce how it represents our victorious breath that helps yogis persevere during challenging flows and asanas.

Perseverance Through Asana

Have students take *Goddess Pose* (Utkata Konasana) or *Horse Pose* (Vatayanasana) with the palms together at the heart center, which allows us to feel confident, powerful, and in charge. Goddess Pose also helps to develop strength that can make other poses easier, such as hip openers and *Warrior* (Virabhadrasana) positions. This fiery asana can be challenging for strength and flexibility—but with perseverance, we can test our strength by coming onto the toes of one foot and then the other, before simultaneously lifting onto the toes of both feet. Once students experience confidence in the pose, they can release by transitioning into a wide-legged forward fold of their choice. Allow them to rest and rejoice in their achievement.

Perseverance can also be tested by holding *High Plank Pose* (Phalakasana) and its variations. These include *Low Plank* (Chaturanga), *Side Plank* (Vasisthasana), and Side Plank with a *Tree Pose* (Vrksasana) leg either above or below the ankle, or a Side Plank while reaching for the lifted foot with the raised hand. Another option is to take *Upward Plank Pose* (Purvottanasana) to consider perseverance from an upward perspective and an open heart.

These poses take resilience and entire body strength to challenge yogis physically and mentally. Thereby, these asanas train students to persevere in other areas of their lives.

More Inspiration on Perseverance

"I have not failed. I've just found 10,000 ways that won't work." – Thomas A. Edison

"There's no value in digging shallow wells in a hundred places. Decide on one place and dig deep. Even if you encounter a rock, use dynamite and keep going down. If you leave that to dig another well, all the first effort is wasted and there is no proof you won't hit rock again." – Swami Satchidananda

"Life doesn't get easier or more forgiving, we get stronger and more resilient." – Steve Maraboli

"Today expect something good to happen to you no matter what occurred yesterday. Realize the past no longer holds you captive. It can only continue to hurt you if you hold on to it. Let the past go. A simply abundant world awaits." – Sarah Ban Breathnach

"You don't learn to walk by following the rules. You learn by doing and falling over." – Richard Branson

"Character consists of what you do on the third and fourth tries." – James A. Michener

"I've always believed that if you put in the work, the results will come." – Michael Jordan

"It's not that I'm so smart. I just stay with problems longer." – Albert Einstein

"I am seeking, I am striving, I am in it with all my heart." – Vincent van Gogh

- ♪ *Progress* – Ever So Blue
- ♪ *Moving* – Eskimotion
- ♪ *Limitations* – East Forest

EMPOWERMENT

Notes

Reassurance

Reassurance means to assist in alleviating doubt and fear. It involves kindness through moral support, which can help others and ourselves to succeed. Reassurance fuels the belief that goals can be achieved and that all will be well. When we offer this to ourselves, we practice self-assurance.

In yoga, props and verbal encouragement provide reassurance to students who might doubt their capabilities or fear trying something new. At the same time, students can learn to reassure themselves and believe in their abilities that often exceed expectations.

Reassurance as an Intention

Have students consider an element of their life where they would appreciate reassurance. For example, this could revolve around any uncertainties they might have about themselves, or an important decision that they recently made or are thinking of making. Allow students to dedicate their practice towards identifying reassurance within themselves and developing confidence that they are following the right path. Thus, this practice fosters self-assurance, in addition to helping them be better equipped and experienced to reassure others.

Centering for Reassurance

Take *Abhaya Mudra* (Have No Fear Gesture), which is a mudra for fearlessness, reassurance, protection, and safety. These qualities are invaluable when practicing self-assurance and reassuring others.

> To take this mudra, the right hand is upright with the palm facing outward and away from the body—as if you were gesturing someone to stop. The left hand can be placed gently on the lap.

EMPOWERMENT

While holding the mudra, have students repeat affirmations, such as the following:

I am making the best decisions for myself; Everything is working out; I am on the right path; I am not afraid to leap; I have no doubts; Strength flows through me; I feel supported by the world; I can achieve my goals; etc.

For additional centering, lead a calming meditation by asking students to let the mind be at ease, release all doubts, and welcome reassurance. Then, incorporate a pranayama exercise by leading students in inhaling confidence and exhaling doubt. Repeat this several times to foster self-assurance.

Poses for Reassurance

To practice reassurance through asana practice, have students practice *Headstand* (Sirsasana) or *Handstand* (Adho Mukha Vrksasana) against a wall. This foundation will help students feel reassured that they will not topple backward because the wall is behind them for support. For students who are new to either position, the wall will reinforce the importance of a strong core and straight spine that supports us throughout each day.

For more advanced students, the wall might offer them an opportunity to try a new inversion variation with additional self-assurance. For example, students can try *the Splits* (Hanumanasana) in a handstand by pressing one foot against the wall, or *Scorpion Pose* (Vrischikasana) while touching the wall behind them with their toes.

Furthermore, reassurance is represented by *Half Moon Pose* (Ardha Chandrasana) and *Extended Triangle Pose* (Utthita Trikonasana). These asanas embody the concept of reassurance because they are standing balances with supported variations to keep the mind and body at ease. In both poses, the lowered hand allows the body to act as a sturdy tripod by resting on the floor or a block. This base against the ground provides comfort that students will not fall if they practice proper alignment. Knowing that the ground or a block is below, students can also try lifting the lowered

arm from the ground to challenge their balance further. For more, students can also try *Twisted/Revolved Half Moon* (Parivrtta Ardha Chandrasana) and *Twisted/Revolved Triangle* (Parivrtta Trikonasana).

Inspiration for Reassurance

"Trust yourself. You know more than you think you do." – Benjamin Spock

"If you think you're too small to have an impact, try going to bed with a mosquito in the room." – Anita Roddick

"The only limit to our realization of tomorrow will be our doubts of today." – Franklin D Roosevelt

"Because one believes in oneself, one doesn't try to convince others. Because one is content with oneself, one doesn't need others' approval. Because one accepts oneself, the whole world accepts him or her." – Lao Tzu

"speak quietly to yourself & promise there will be better days. whisper gently to yourself and provide assurance that you really are extending your best effort. console your bruised and tender spirit with reminders of many other successes. offer comfort in practical and tangible ways—as if you were encouraging your dearest friend. recognize that on certain days the greatest grace is that the day is over and you get to close your eyes. tomorrow comes more brightly..." – Mary Anne Radmacher

"In times of stress, the best thing we can do for each other is to listen with our ears and our hearts and to be assured that our questions are just as important as our answers." – Fred Rogers

- ♪ *Self-Assured* – Louis Landon
- ♪ *Reassuring Drops* – Jes Nil
- ♪ *Haseya* – Ajeet, Peia

EMPOWERMENT

Notes

Self-Confidence

Self-confidence is about believing in oneself, being comfortable with who one is, and being certain of their abilities and future. It also requires not underestimating one's abilities. Self-confidence does not require that we are confident all of the time, but that we are confident when we deserve to be—and we deserve to be more often than we might think.

Yoga is an excellent way to understand when it is appropriate to be confident. This is because returning yoga students continue to improve their practice and deserve opportunities to try new poses and techniques while believing that these activities are accessible. Thus, a yoga class surrounding the theme of self-confidence can offer students a chance to recognize deserved confidence within themselves.

Self-Confidence as an Intention

Have students consider where they would like to experience more confidence—whether that relates to sending in an application, awaiting an evaluation, asking for something, or approaching someone. Then, have students consider why they are deserving of success. Encourage students to set an intention to become more confident.

Centering for Self-Confidence

Ganesha Mudra (Remover of Obstacles) builds self-confidence and courage while helping to face difficult situations. It also fosters respect and compassion. The mudra is named after the deity Ganesha, who is said to remove obstacles that stand in our way of achievement.

> To take the two-handed mudra, place the right palm face-up and place the left-hand face-down on top. Clasp the fingers together like hooks.

Holding the mudra, have students repeat confidence affirmations, such as the following:

> *I deserve to be confident; I believe in myself; I am confident in who I am; I dare myself to take the next step; I am equipped to handle anything that comes my way;* etc.

Further, consider leading students in a pranayama exercise that might put them outside of their comfort zone. *Lion's Breath* is an appropriate option because it can feel a bit unnatural and silly—but like yoga in general, this pranayama technique is about a feeling rather than concerning oneself with how they look or sound. This technique also encourages self-confidence because it helps the body and mind feel happier and more energized.

Self-Confidence Through Asana

Take *Mountain Pose* (Tadasana), which is an empowering pose to boost self-confidence. Have students feel their feet and toes stuck to the mat, the spine lengthened, the crown of the head lifted to the sky, and the heart open as the shoulders draw down the back and towards one another. In this asana, ask students to feel strong, empowered, and supported by the earth beneath them. Have them feel cemented to the ground while holding their heads high with inner confidence.

For more, Mountain Pose can be transitioned into an *Upward Salute* (Urdhva Hastasana) by reaching the hands towards the sky while gazing upwards, or into *Standing Side Stretches* (Parsva Urdhva Hastasana) to extend the side-body. These variations also represent how self-confidence begins with a strong and grounded base and our ability to work alongside the force of gravity. Mention how true self-confidence is built from the ground up.

More Inspiration on Self-Confidence

"The world stands aside to let anyone pass who knows where he is going." – David Starr Jordan

"The root of true confidence grows from unconditional friendship with ourselves, to train in gentleness, and to trust in our natural intelligence to navigate life." – Pema Chodron

"Be who you are and say what you feel, because those who mind don't matter and those who matter don't mind." – Dr Seuss

"Don't be satisfied with stories, how things have gone with others. Unfold your own myth." – Rumi

"The moment you doubt whether you can fly, you cease forever to be able to do it." – J.M. Barrie

"Look well into thyself; there is a source of strength which will always spring up if thou wilt always look." – Marcus Aurelius

- ♪ *Strength From Inside* – Above & Beyond
- ♪ *Road* – Lane 8, Arctic Lake
- ♪ *I Am* – Fia

Notes

V. INFINITE OPPORTUNITIES

"Define success on your own terms, achieve it by your own rules, and build a life you're proud to live"

— Ann Sweeney

Opportunities surround us whether or not we always recognize them. While some people experience more options throughout their lives than others, and we are faced with different circumstances, everyone has choices that can direct their future for the better. Thus, this chapter introduces yoga class themes that recognize and embrace endless opportunities that exist for everyone. The themes in this chapter help to reveal new horizons for the future and help to gain a new appreciation for boundless innate resources that we might overlook.

This chapter addresses five yoga class themes that act as inspiration to recognize and utilize our infinite opportunities: Agency, Exploration, Journey, Perspective, and Positive Habits.

The theme of *Agency* emphasizes our ability to choose and make decisions for ourselves. *Exploration* through yoga involves connecting to our endless curiosity. *Journey* recognizes our different paths and teaches us to be more cognizant of opportunities that appear along the way. *Perspective* encourages us to consider circumstances from different points of view, thereby finding opportunities when we might not otherwise recognize them. And the class theme surrounding *Positive Habits* helps us use yoga as a tool for overcoming addictions or creating a healthier everyday lifestyle.

These themes relating to infinite opportunities are explored through descriptions, centering exercises, pose recommendations, and inspirational material that help to connect your personalized classes to your modern yoga students.

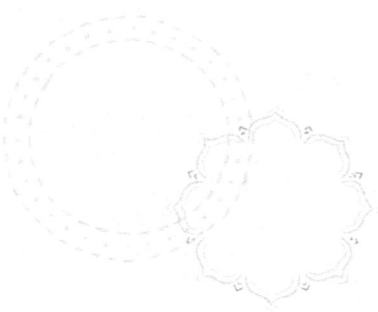

Agency

Agency is our power to choose and determine our own path. Thus, agency is our ability to make decisions for ourselves. It also relates to our innate independence and freedom to be who we want to be. The fact that we have agency means that we have control over our lives and are free to make our own choices. With this power, we should not restrain ourselves while also making sure to make the best decisions for ourselves and responsible decisions that affect others.

Yoga can help modern yogis to act upon their agency by allowing them to take modifications for their bodies and to choose what classes to attend, for example. Students can also choose anything from the spot they unroll their mat, to their unique practice intention.

Agency as an Intention

Have students consider how they might feel restraint in their life. Remind students that they have the power to guide their own future and make decisions that will benefit them. Open their minds to their unlimited agency and let that guide their practice. As such, have them form an intention to embrace their ability to choose and to be their own agents.

Centering with Agency

Take *Karana Mudra* (Instrument Gesture), which represents how our bodies are instruments by which we process karma. Thus, this mudra recognizes that we have a powerful sense of agency within us while inspiring us to practice good behavior and make virtuous decisions— including being compassionate and understanding of others.

> To practice this mudra, take the 'rock on' gesture by touching the nails of the ring and middle fingers to the back of the thumb, while extending the little and pointer fingers upwards.

While holding Karana Mudra, encourage students to repeat agency-inspired affirmations in their heads, such as the following:

I have the power to be who I want to be; My life is full of opportunity; I make my own decisions with confidence; I offer myself the ability to choose; etc.

Also, consider allowing students to practice agency through a simple meditation and pranayama exercises by focusing on their own *home base* and choosing whether to exhale through their mouth or nose. Provide a few examples of home base options, such as the breath or a specific spot such as the third eye, belly button, or heart space. Highlighting choices for students helps to tap into a sense of agency by encouraging students to make their own decisions that feel best for them.

Remind students that *prana* means life energy and *ayama* means control—highlighting that they have control and agency over their breath.

Agency Through Asana

Lead students into *Boat Pose* (Navasana), which represents our bodies as boats on an open and limitless body of water. With our own sails, we have the ability to direct our everyday lives despite any waves and winds that challenge our direction. Thus, Boat Pose represents our inherent agency.

Boat Pose also allows us to practice agency because it has several variations, including keeping palms on the ground, keeping shins and arms parallel to the ground, straightening the legs, and eventually guiding the feet higher and the body onto the thighs into *Upward-Facing West Intense Stretch Pose* (Urdhva Mukha Paschimottanasana). Encourage students to practice their agency by taking variations that suit them at the time.

More Inspiration on Agency

"We cannot direct the wind, but we can adjust the sails." – Dolly Parton

"If you are distressed by anything external, the pain is not due to the thing itself, but to your estimate of it; and this you have the power to revoke at any moment." – Marcus Aurelius

"It is our choices that show what we truly are, far more than our abilities." – J.K. Rowling

"I am no bird; and no net ensnares me: I am a free human being with an independent will." – Charlotte Brontë

"We have little power to choose what happens, but we have complete power over how we respond." – Arianna Huffington

"The best way to control cow and sheep is to give them a big grazing field." – Shunryu Suzuki"

"The freedom of Mankind does not lie in the fact that we can do what we want, but that we do not have to do that which we do not want." – Jean Jacques Rousseau

"If you do what you've always done, you'll get what you've always gotten." – Tony Robbins

- ♪ *Goodness* – Emancipator
- ♪ *Home Again* – Drala
- ♪ *Want Me* – Affalaye

YOGA THEMES FOR MODERN YOGIS

Notes

Exploration

Exploration is our ability to search, learn, discover or travel. Through exploring, we continue to discover more about our universe and we fuel our endless curiosity and a continued sense of adventure.

No matter where we are or what we have, we always have the ability to explore. Exploration does not require a passport or money. Rather, we can educate ourselves through books and the internet, ask questions, go for walks and observe the surroundings, and take a closer look at the little things that already exist in our lives.

Moreover, we can practice exploration through yoga. For example, there will always be a new asana variation or meditation technique that students can try. A modern yoga class inspired by the theme of exploration can encourage students to try new things, get out of their comfort zone, and feel exhilarated. As such, these experiences can be translated to exploration in their lives outside of the class setting.

Exploration as an Intention

Allow students to enter a mentality of exploration. They might brainstorm where they would like to explore. This could be a city, a museum, a library, or a park, for example. Then, have them consider what they would like to explore when they get there—whether that is something they can study, wander through, or reflect on. Notice the feelings of excitement that arise and have that energy inspire their practice. Encourage them to set an intention to continue exploring.

Centering for Exploration

Take *Garuda Mudra* (Eagle Gesture), which is said to help us explore new possibilities. The eagle is also a symbol of protection and ease during exploration.

To take the mudra, splay all ten fingers and bring them towards your heart with palms facing towards you and interlock the thumbs. The mudra shape resembles open eagle wings.

Keeping the hands in Garuda Mudra, have students repeat exploration-themed affirmations, such as the following:

I am passionate about learning and trying new things; I act on my curiosity; I will never stop exploring; etc.

As an explorative take on pranayama, have students place one hand on their chest and the other on their belly. Have them feel their chest rise and fall for a few breaths before having them focus on keeping their chest still while expanding and contracting their belly.

Further, you might incorporate *Kapalabhati* pranayama (skull-cleansing breath), whereby exhales become forced and inhales become more passive. This breathing pattern is the opposite of our natural breath; therefore, it allows us to explore something out of the ordinary.

Exploration through Poses

Exploration is represented by *Extended Side-Angle* (Utthita Parsvakonasana) because it has numerous variations that allow us to experience different sensations throughout our bodies while maintaining the same grounding, leg positioning, and core stability.

For example, in a traditional side angle, the hand on the ground can be placed on either side of the front foot and the hand can be raised, extended over the head, or clasped into a bind behind the back. It can also be turned into a twist by placing the opposite hand down on either side of the front foot. Moreover, it can be used as a warmup by incorporating alternating opening and twisting variations with the front knee lifted from the ground.

Overall, yoga itself is about exploration and curiosity, and it gives us endless possibilities for exploring what our bodies can do. Be inspired to invent new variations and play with creative transitions.

More Inspiration for Exploration

"Twenty years from now you will be more disappointed by the things that you didn't do than by the ones you did do. So throw off the bowlines. Sail away from the safe harbor. Catch the trade winds in your sails. Explore. Dream. Discover." – H. Jackson Brown Jr.

"And the end of all our exploring/ Will be to arrive where we started/ And know the place for the first time." – T.S. Eliot

"We sometimes need to lose sight of our priorities in order to see them." – John Irving

"Not all those who wander are lost." – J.R.R. Tolkien

"Man cannot discover new oceans unless he has the courage to lose sight of the shore." – J. Andre Gide

"We need the tonic of wildness...At the same time that we are earnest to explore and learn all things, we require that all things be mysterious and unexplorable, that land and sea be indefinitely wild, unsurveyed and unfathomed by us because unfathomable. We can never have enough of nature." – Henry David Thoreau

"We have an unknown distance yet to run, an unknown river to explore." – John Wesley Powell

- ♪ *They Move on Tracks of Never-Ending Light* – This Will Destroy You
- ♪ *Om Ganesha* – Mose, Sam Garrett
- ♪ *Moon River* – Frank Ocean
- ♪ *Lost in The Night* – Palace

YOGA THEMES FOR MODERN YOGIS

Notes

Journey

A journey is the act of traveling, and it is characterized by our experiences along the way. It is what happens as we move from point A to point B—which can be physical locations or a figurative construct for working from a starting place and in the direction of certain achievements.

Yoga can help us to understand the philosophical concept of a journey, which represents and encourages us to appreciate various stages in our lives. We can do this by working towards specific goals while taking time to note and appreciate the little achievements, emotions, and sensations along the way. By doing so, we can be better equipped to appreciate our everyday journeys—no matter where they lead or reroute.

Journey as an Intention

Have students consider a personal journey and where they hope to arrive, or have recently arrived. Have them note something that they enjoyed that happened along the way, such as a milestone or celebration. Let this reinforce the importance of enjoying a journey and encourage students to set an intention to appreciate the sequence of experiences throughout their lives more than focusing exclusively on the destinations.

Journey-Themed Centering

Take *Ashvaratna Mudra* (Horse-Jewel Gesture) to explore new situations, choices, and perspectives. It also strengthens observational skills, eliminates narrowmindedness, and counteracts negative behavioral patterns. These are all assets for an enjoyable journey.

> To take the two-handed mudra, bring the hands together in a prayer-like position with the fingers splayed apart—one side mirroring the other. Lower and clasp the pointer and middle fingers onto the knuckles.

Maintaining the mudra, have students repeat journey-inspired affirmations like the following:

> *My life is an exciting and ongoing journey; I cherish the little moments; I celebrate my achievements; I shine a light on the right path;* etc.

Then, lead students in a *day trip* meditation by imagining a beautiful location that they are traveling towards. Have them consider how they are getting there, who they are traveling with, and what they are doing to stay occupied along the way. Students might realize that the journey becomes more interesting than the destination that they originally had in mind—and this represents the journeys that we experience every day.

Journey Through Poses

Have students take *Bridge Pose* (Setu Bandha Sarvangasana) because it represents the bridges between life events that we continue to cross. The asana also represents how our bodies are bridges themselves that support us throughout life's journey.

Moreover, Bridge Pose can be a transitional asana into *Wheel/Upward Bow Pose* (Urdhva Dhanurasana). Wheel Pose symbolizes the wheel of life with various stages of progression. It also represents a high bridge over the obstacles of life's journeys. Variations include working towards straightening the legs, walking the hands and feet closer to one another, and lifting one leg at a time. Students might enter and exit Wheel through a standing transition.

Further, you can teach poses that require numerous steps. Options include working toward *King Pigeon* (Eka Pada Rajakapotasana), *Twisted Triangle* (Parivrtta Trikonasana) variations, or *Side Crow Pose* (Parsva Bakasana).

More Journey Inspiration

"[T]he joy of travel is not nearly so much in getting where one wants to go as in the unsought surprises which occur on the journey." — Alan W. Watts

"In yoga we are interested in how we go, not how far we go." — Mark Stephens

"As you walk, eat and travel, be where you are. Otherwise, you will miss most of your life." — Gautama Buddha

"Life is about accepting the challenges along the way, choosing to keep moving forward, and savoring the journey." — Roy T. Bennett

"It is good to have an end to journey toward; but it is the journey that matters, in the end." — Ursula K. Le Guin

- ♪ *The Lost Words Blessing* — The Lost Words: Spell Songs, Julie Fowlis, et al.
- ♪ *Voyage* — Eric Wilhelm
- ♪ *Journey of the Monarch* — Christi Stills
- ♪ *On the Road Again* — PIAMINO
- ♪ *The Journey* — Sol Rising

Notes

Perspective

Perspective is one's viewpoint, perception, or a particular way of considering something. For example, one might have a positive or negative outlook, or they might automatically consider something in a certain light because of bias or preconception. Perspective can also be shaped by a long-term mindset or a train of thought that can change. Still, perspectives can evolve.

Perspective is a beautiful concept to explore through yoga because both practices involve understanding varying points of view that allow us to look at the world differently and rekindle a sense of wonder and emotional intelligence. Perspective can also help us to become more compassionate and generous.

Yoga classes can shape a positive perspective by creating a comfortable environment that is conducive to a healthy lifestyle and positive mood. Yoga encourages us to be open-minded and open to changing the way we think about mental health, spirituality, and the body. These considerations help us to become better versions of ourselves who are more cognizant and appreciative of the world.

Perspective as an Intention

Have students think about a recent disagreement or a recent time that they were displeased with someone. Then, have them consider something about that instance that they might understand—even if they still disagree. This class is about becoming more understanding by challenging our point-of-view, which is achieved through exploring new perspectives in yoga. Accordingly, allow students to set an intention to challenge their perspective in order to observe life through a more positive lens.

Perspective Centering

Take *Chin Mudra* (Unrestricted Consciousness Gesture) with one hand and *Jnana/Gyana Mudra* (Wisdom Gesture) with the other. Chin Mudra is said to help expand the consciousness and Gyana Mudra taps into intuitive knowledge. Together, these mudras represent perspective because they involve the same finger positioning but have different benefits depending on whether the palm is faced down (Guana Mudra) or up (Chin Mudra).

> To take these mudras, extend the pinky, ring, and middle fingers slightly apart while tucking the index finger into the crease of the thumb to form an oval shape.

Have students repeat affirmations for perspective, such as the following:

> *I challenge myself to see things from different perspectives; I choose to understand things from others' points of view; I choose optimism and positive interpretations;* etc.

During other meditation exercises, have students close their eyes and focus on their third eye, or look through closed eyelids. This practice encourages students to consider vision through a new perspective, rather than through their standard sense of sight. Have them consider what colors, shapes, and visions they might see.

Asanas for Perspective

To allow students to challenge their perspective through yoga poses, have them practice inversions. Options include *Headstand* (Sirsasana), *Candlestick* (Supta Dandasana), *Shoulder Stand* (Salamba Sarvangasana), and *Plow Pose* (Halasana) by lowering the legs behind the head from Shoulder Stand. These poses redirect blood flow and allow students to experience their practice space from a new point of view.

You might have students also take *Eagle Pose (Garudasana)* from different perspectives. These include the traditional twisted standing balance on one foot, or a reclined variation on the back with the option of incorporating knee-to-elbow crunches. Eagle Pose can also be taken and upside-down while in a Headstand.

Furthermore, students can take *Upward Plank Pose* (Purvottanasana) that flips our perspective from a *High Plank pose* (Phalakasana). Upward Plank requires similar arm and core strength but opens the heart and neck to the sky to feel a release across the chest and throat.

More Inspiration on Perspective

"Some people feel the rain, others just get wet." – Bob Marley

"Even the stones placed in one's path can be made into something beautiful." – Goethe

"Everyone is a genius. But if you judge a fish by its ability to climb a tree, it will live its whole life believing that it is stupid." – Albert Einstein

"Weeds are flowers too when you get to know them." – A.A. Milne

"When you change how you look at things, the things you look at change." – Wayne Dyer

"The real voyage of discovery consists not in seeking new landscapes, but in having new eyes." – Marcel Proust

"An optimist does not stand in the rain; he is taking a shower under a cloud." – Thomas Romanus

"Notice that the stiffest tree is most easily cracked, while the bamboo or willow survives by bending with the wind." – Bruce Lee

- ♪ *Sunlight In The Night* – Martin Gauffin
- ♪ *Both Sides Now* – Joni Mitchell
- ♪ *Lace* – Random Rab

INFINITE OPPORTUNITIES

Notes

Positive Habits

A habit is a recurring tendency or practice. Negative and unwanted habits, such as addictions, can be difficult to break and give up. On the other hand, positive habits require time to establish and we are often reluctant to commit to the repetition that is required to ensure these become second nature or part of a lifestyle change.

This modern yoga class is about focusing on positive habits—whether that is working towards establishing a new routine, or working towards eliminating an unwanted addiction. Positive habits are developed by committing to change and establishing constructive alterations in one's life. Moreover, introducing new positive habits can also help to negate negative habits, such as going for regular walks when you are used to watching television.

Positive Habits as an Intention

Have students consider something new that they would like to incorporate into their daily or weekly lives or a habit that they wish to break. Give examples, such as eating cleaner, becoming less wasteful, having less screen time, or giving up a vice. Have them dedicate this practice towards nurturing a mindset of breaking bad habits and finding motivation within themselves to initiate positive change.

Centering to Encourage Better Habits

Take *Kaleswara Mudra* (Lord of Time Gesture), which helps to calm the mind and eliminate addictive behaviors and patterns. Thus, this mudra helps to cleanse and purify the mind in order to guide in making better and more positive habits.

> To take this mudra, make a heart shape with the hands by placing both fists together and extending the thumbs downwards. Maintaining this shape, extend the middle fingers upwards.

While holding Kaleswara Mudra, have students repeat affirmations to encourage positive habits, such as the following:

> *I can make positive changes in my life; consistency comes from experience; change takes consistency; routines take practice*; etc.

Furthermore, lead students in *Nadi Shodhana* pranayama (alternate nostril breathing), which helps us challenge the habit of breathing through only one nostril. Begin by having students place a finger underneath their nose and notice which side of the nose releases more air. After repeating Nadi Shodhana for at least eight rounds, have students notice a more even distribution of air releasing from both nostrils at once. This practice represents our ability to make positive changes and create greater balance in our lives if we practice repetition.

Poses for Positive Habits

In this practice, reinforce the importance of alignment. This is essential for creating good habits, which will become second nature in a long-term yoga practice and will allow us to continue attempting new challenges.

For beginner and intermediate students, you might dedicate time to *Low Plank* (Chaturanga). This asana is often flowed through without giving proper attention to alignment. By breaking down this pose, you will encourage students to get out of old habits and focus on the true integrity of the pose. Try incorporating Chaturanga pushups by transitioning between *High Plank pose* (Phalakasana) and Low Plank while paying attention to the different muscle engagements and shoulder alignment. To prevent the elbows from drawing outwards, you can also have students incorporate the use of props by tightening a strap around the outside of both biceps.

Furthermore, a class surrounding positive habits can pay special attention to the integrity of forward folds—incorporating symmetrical asanas like *Standing Forward Bend* (Uttanasana) and *Seated Forward Bend* (Paschimottanasana). To do this, remind students to bend at the hips and keep a bend in their knees if the torso does not reach the thighs with a lengthened spine. Revisiting these habits will protect the spine long term and will encourage an organic development of flexibility from the toes to the cervical spine and the fingertips.

For more advanced students, you might review alignments for more challenging positions, such as *Handstand* (Adho Mukha Vrksasana) and *Head Stand* (Sirsasana) with drills against a wall. For difficult positions like these, yogis can sometimes neglect technique when trying to make a pose look a certain way. Thus, have students revisit their intentions and have those encourage them to practice positive habits in yoga for a healthy body and mind.

Inspiration for Encouraging Positive Habits

"You'll never change your life unless you change something you do daily. The secret to your success is found in your daily routine." – John C Maxwell

"We are addicted to our thoughts. We cannot change anything if we cannot change our thinking." – Santosh Kalwar

"We are what we repeatedly do. Excellence, then, is not an act, but a habit." – Will Durant

"Remember that this is not something we do just once or twice. Interrupting our destructive habits and awakening our heart is the work of a lifetime." – Pema Chödrön

"Mere philosophy will not satisfy us. We cannot reach the goal by mere words alone. Without practice, nothing can be achieved." – Swami Satchidananda

- ♪ *With Resolve* – Jacob Yoffee
- ♪ *Routine* – Green Haze
- ♪ *You Can't Rush Your Healing* – Trevor Hall

INFINITE OPPORTUNITIES

Notes

VI. SELF-APPRECIATION

*"Self-appreciation is a sign of maturity,
seeking appreciation is a sign of immaturity"*

— Sivaprakash Sidhu

We are all prone to comparing ourselves to others and undermining ourselves in the process. We might observe someone who has a lifestyle, quality, characteristic, or material item that we desire or envy, and we lose appreciation for what we have and who we are. Thus, this chapter addresses how modern yoga classes can encourage transformative experiences that help us to release our judgmental mindsets and embrace our admirable qualities. Through yoga, we can nourish our self-appreciation and self-recognition—thereby becoming more radiant and confident individuals.

This chapter outlines four essential yoga class themes that encourage us to appreciate more about ourselves: Affirmation, Authenticity, Life, and Self-Love. The theme of *Affirmation* encourages us to highlight and embrace the positive qualities within ourselves. *Authenticity* through yoga encourages us to appreciate the unique qualities that make us special and important to the world. Next, the theme of *Life* encourages us to recognize the invaluable and infinitely special gift of simply being on this earth. And the yoga class theme of *Self-Love* inspires us to admire ourselves as unique and beautiful individuals.

SELF-APPRECIATION

All of these self-appreciative themes are presented with reference to mindfulness exercises, asana suggestions, and inspirational resources in order to plan meaningful classes for contemporary yoga students.

Affirmation

An affirmation is a positive assertion. It is about building confidence and feeling grounded within ourselves. Affirmations help us to counter doubts and underestimation of ourselves, and they provide self-encouragement and self-appreciation.

An affirmation theme can be incorporated into modern yoga classes as a way to build upon the importance of confidence and self-love for believing in ourselves and appreciating who we are. A class of this nature incorporates uplifting mantras throughout the class to connect with modern yoga students.

Affirmation as an Intention

Have students consider an element of their life that could improve if they had greater trust in themselves, such as a project they are working on, a path they would like to follow, or a positive quality that they would like to highlight. Give them a moment to consider how this goal can inspire a personalized affirmation for their intention and practice. For example, they might select a simple mantra like 'I am good enough' or 'I am brave' in relation to their lives.

Centering with Affirmation

Take *Bhu Mudra* (Touching the Earth Gesture), which represents stability, patience, and perseverance in achieving goals. It allows us to feel grounded and confident, which is essential for affirming our path.

> To take the mudra, make a peace sign with the right hand and rest that hand on the thigh or knee with the palm facing down.

Holding Bhu Mudra, have students take affirmations, such as the following:

> *I trust my intuition; I honor myself; I am the best guide to my future; I am headed down the right path; every decision I make is the right one for me*; etc.

Another option is to encourage students to repeat their personalized affirmation or mantra that reflects their practice intention. Have students repeat this in their heads several times.

Another centering option is to guide students to close their eyes for meditation and tune into their practice intention. Have students visualize how their life might look when they achieve their goal, and take note of the positivity they feel. Keeping this vision in mind, have students breathe in self-belief and exhale negative energy and everything inconsistent with their intention.

Affirmation through Poses

Take *Cow Face Pose* (Gomukhasana) that connects us to the ground, opens the heart, and helps us to understand the anatomy that is authentic to us. With the use of props, it can be an accessible asana for anyone—allowing everyone to find a position that honors their intention. The full seated pose involves stacking the knees on top of one another and clasping the hands behind the back. Students might feel comfortable using their shirt or a strap behind their backs if they experience tightness. Or, they might lead the upper arm down between the shoulder blades by guiding it at the elbow with the opposite hand. Further, they might use bolsters or blankets to sit on or support the knees, or they might take any seated position that they find comfortable. Have students sit tall and proud in their committed position.

Another alternative or a transition from Cow Face pose is *Half Lord of the Fishes Pose/Seated Twist Pose* (Ardha Matsyendrasana). This opens the chest with pride while massaging the spine that represents the body's foundation and support structure. It also allows the hands and legs to release after having bound the hands in Cow Face. Have students reflect upon their achievements and focus on future successes.

Also consider having students explore the significance of other grounding and self-affirming positions, such as *Tree Pose* (Vrksasana) with confidently outstretched arms as branches and an unmoving *Mountain Pose* (Tadasana).

More Inspiration on Affirmation

"The man who thinks he can and the man who thinks he can't are both right." – Confucius

"It's the repetition of affirmation that leads to belief. And once that belief becomes a deep conviction, things begin to happen." – Muhammed Ali

"Once you make a decision, the universe conspires to make it happen." – Ralph Waldo Emmerson

"Life teaches us the right path is rarely the easy one." – Roy T. Bennett

"What we think about and thank about is what we bring about." – Rhonda Byrne

"No need to hurry. No need to sparkle. No need to be anybody but oneself." – Virginia Woolf

- ♪ *Sweet Disposition* – Kirsten Agresta Copely
- ♪ *I am the Light of My Soul* – Andi Flax
- ♪ *Steady as Stone* – Steady as Stone
- ♪ *I Am* – Nirinjan Kaur, Matthew Schoening

SELF-APPRECIATION

Notes

Authenticity

To be authentic means to be genuine and original. Authenticity relates to our character, personality, and who we are at our core. Sometimes being authentic takes courage, but it honors ourselves and opens our hearts to others.

Yoga encourages us to be our authentic selves through self-expression and appreciating the best versions of who we are. Thus, a yoga class dedicated to the theme of authenticity encourages us to be truer to ourselves and cherishes our identity in order to live a happier and healthier life.

Authenticity as an Intention

Have students consider how they can better embrace their authentic and unique personalities throughout their daily lives. Have them dedicate their yoga practice towards authenticity by not holding back an expression and allowing their positive energy to illuminate the space around them.

Centering with Authenticity

Take *Mushtika Mudra* (Joined Fist Offering), which represents self-appreciation and authenticity. In this mudra, have students imagine a precious jewel inside their hands that is representative of their unique talents, gifts, and sincerity. These are authentic and beautiful qualities of oneself that must be treated with care and respect.

> To take this two-handed mudra, bring the finger pads of the first four fingers down towards the heels of the hands while keeping the thumbs facing up. Then, press the hands together, meeting at the backside of the finger joints and keeping the thumbs parallel.

Repeat affirmations for authenticity, such as the following:

> *I am beautiful because I am unique; I am one-of-a-kind; I express my authentic self; I am shamelessly myself; I am true to myself and others; I am not afraid to express who I am;* etc.

For a simple meditation and pranayama practice, allow students to focus on their authentic breath without trying to control it. Take note of how it sounds and how it feels. Have them consider how air contacts their throat and expands the lungs, ribs, and belly. Remind them to just observe and appreciate their authentic breath, or *prana*, that has given them life.

Authenticity through Poses & Movement

To explore the concept of authenticity, allow students to play with their hip mobility and increase the intensity of stretches to their level of comfort. You might begin with a *Wide-Legged Forward Bend* (Prasarita Padottanasana I) with the option to hold the hips, touch the floor, walk the hands behind, or take a twist. Another option is a *Yogi Squat* (Malasana) with or without sitting on a block, and a *Goddess Pose* (Utkata Konasana) that can be taken with various arm positions and with or without coming onto the toes of either or both feet. Then allow students to play with *Side Lunge Pose* (Skandasana) with the options touch the floor, keep the hands in a prayer position, open the arms like an airplane, open the knees with the forearms to intensify the stretch, or take a bind.

By playing with hip flexibility, modern yoga students can take note of their unique anatomy and can move intuitively as they play with their complex hip joints and discover new mobility.

Another pose for authenticity is a *Low Crescent Lunge* (Anjaneyasana), which has the option to lean back to touch blocks or the floor behind or to bend the back knee to grab the back foot. Invite students to consider how each side feels different at their own pace.

Mention that students might choose to incorporate a bind. Have them take any modifications or more challenging variations that their bodies ask for at the time.

More Inspiration on Authenticity

"Never apologize for being yourself." – Paulo Coelho

"The biggest challenge in life is to be yourself in a world that is trying to make you like everyone else." – Ralph Waldo Emerson

"Today you are You. That is truer than true. There is no-one alive who is Youer than You." – Dr Suess

"We have to dare to be ourselves, however frightening or strange that self may prove to be." – May Sarton

"According to this law [the law of Dharma], you have a unique talent and a unique way of expressing it. There is something that you can do better than anyone else in the whole world--and for every unique talent and unique expression of that talent, there are also unique needs. When these needs are matched with the creative expression of your talent, that is the spark that creates affluence. Expressing your talents to fulfill needs creates unlimited wealth and abundance." – Deepak Chopra

- ♪ *Talk is Cheap* – Chet Faker
- ♪ *And Then I Woke Up* – Idealism
- ♪ *This Feeling* – Alabama Shakes

SELF-APPRECIATION

Notes

Life

Life is the experience of being alive, whereby our everyday experiences define our existence. All life—every person and every living thing—has beauty and deserves to be appreciated. Think of all of the things we have been able to do and accomplish, how we have been able to love, and all the tangible and intangible things we are able to appreciate in the world.

Applying the concept of life as a class theme helps to encourage students to appreciate life as a precious gift. No matter what occurs throughout our lifetimes, we still exist and have opportunities and relationships that shape who we are and who we can be in the future. These elements can be appreciated through yoga by acknowledging what we are capable of achieving and how the practice helps us to live a healthier life in mind, body, and spirit.

Life as an Intention

Encourage students to set an intention that honors their own life. For example, an intention might revolve around opportunities that they appreciate, accomplishments that they are proud of, or qualities that they love about themselves. Encourage students to take time to truly appreciate themselves and their unlimited value.

Students can also suggest dedicating the class to the life of someone that they know, the lives of others, or other living things in the natural world.

Life-Themed Centering

Take *Prana Mudra* (Life Force Gesture or Energy Seal), which activates dormant energy and encourages the flow of energy to feel strong and alive. This mudra is said to strengthen the immune system, increase vitality, and invigorate the body. Thus, Prana Mudra honors life.

To take this mudra, make a peace sign, connecting the thumb with the pinky and ring fingers while extending the middle and index fingers together side-by-side. Allow the palms to face up while resting the backside of the hands on the thighs. You may take this with both hands.

Guide the class in repeating life-themed affirmations, such as the following:

Life is filled with abundance and joy; I love my life; All life is sacred; I respect all living things; I honor myself; I respect others; etc.

Furthermore, reintroduce the concept of pranayama to students to underscore the necessity of breath for life. Remind students that *prana* is defined as breath and life energy—meaning that breath is our primary energy and life source. Then, review *Ujjayi* pranayama, which encourages us to practice victorious breathing that celebrates our life energy.

Life-Inspired Asanas

Take poses that represent and honor life. For example, these can be child-inspired poses, such as *Child's Pose* (Balasana), *Happy Baby Pose* (Ananda Balasana), and *One-Leg Baby Cradle*. These draw us back to the beginning of our existence and help us to appreciate all that life has allowed us to achieve.

Similarly, allow students to transition from *Corpse Pose* (Savasana) into a fetal position for several breaths. Highlight how this represents the birth of a new day and fresh mindset after their yoga practice.

You might also focus on poses that represent growth in life, such as *Tree Pose* (Vrksasana). In Tree Pose, have students reach towards the sun, which gives the earth life, and imagine tree roots offering them stability. Encourage students to connect with the natural world around them.

More Inspiration for Life

"Find ecstasy in life, the mere sense of living is joy enough." – Emily Dickenson

"To live is the rarest thing in the world. Most people exist, that is all." – Oscar Wilde

"The two most important days in your life are the day you are born, and the day you find out why." – Zen Proverb

"The success of yoga does not lie in the ability to perform postures but in how it positively changes the way we live our life and our relationships." – T.K.V. Desikachar

"Dance like nobody's watching. Love like you've never been hurt. Sing like nobody's listening. Live like it's heaven on earth." – Mark Twain

"Life is what happens while you're busy making other plans." – John Lennon

"Yoga is like music: the rhythm of the body, the melody of the mind, and the harmony of the soul create the symphony of life." – B.K.S. Iyengar

"Living well is an art that can be developed: a love of life and ability to take great pleasure from small offerings and assurance that the world owes you nothing and that every gift is exactly that, a gift." – Maya Angelou

- ♪ *The Circle Game* – Joni Mitchell
- ♪ *The Fawn* – Goetz Oestlind
- ♪ *Gayatri Mantra Without Rhythm* – Jagit Singh
- ♪ *Hummingbird* – Miss E

SELF-APPRECIATION

Notes

Self-Love

Self-love is about unconditionally appreciating and loving yourself, which is essential for living a happy life. Self-love honors our relationship with ourselves and allows us to love others with a full heart.

Sometimes, it is easier to criticize the negative characteristics of ourselves than appreciate the positive ones, and yoga helps to prevent these thoughts. A self-love yoga practice is about focusing on positivity while recognizing what makes us imperfect and finding self-love regardless. Moreover, a self-love-themed class should enforce how we should move intuitively, do what feels best, and explore our true selves.

Self-Love as an Intention

Have students begin by thinking about the people that they love and who might be at the top of that list and who might be further down the line. Have students consider how long down the list they would name themselves.

Then, explain how this practice should inspire them to return to the top of the list. Without oneself, one cannot love others to the best of one's abilities. In this vein, have students focus their practice on loving themselves and making that a priority. Allow them to feel at home within themselves.

Centering with Self-Love

Take *Mrit Sanjeevani Mudra* (Lifesaving Gesture), which benefits the heart and lungs, encourages self-care and reflection, in addition to slowing down to benefit the mind and body—thereby encouraging self-love.

> To take this mudra, tuck the index finger under the thumb, pinch the thumb, ring, and middle fingers together, and extend the pinky finger.

Self-love affirmations can be among the most powerful and transformative, so select them with heartfelt intentions. Examples include the following:

> *I love myself and who I am; I am kind, loving, and patient with myself; I love who I have been and who I will become; I am worth loving; There is love all around me; Love is always here for me*; etc.

As a simple centering meditation, have students close their eyes and focus on inhaling self-love and exhaling all resentment towards oneself. Repeat this for several rounds. Pause afterward and enjoy their radiating positivity.

Poses for Self-Love

A simple self-love asana is a *Reclined Hug* (Apanasana). Spend time in this pose by curling up tighter, or loosening the hug to flatten the spine. This can also be transitioned into relaxing spinal twists to give love to the spine that supports our bodies.

Apanasana can also transition into *Bridge Pose* (Setu Bandha Sarvangasana) to open our hearts, *Candlestick/Reclined Staff Pose* (Supta Dandasana) to burn brighter, *Reclined Butterfly* (Supta Baddha Konasana) to release tension from the hips, and *Corpse Pose* (Savasana) to completely let go and relax. All of these poses respect the body and encourage self-love by allowing it to move in healthy ways. Have students indulge in every pose.

You might also select heart-opening poses, such as Camel Pose (Ustrasana) to encourage a release of tension and stagnant energy in the heart space, which can help to give and receive love for oneself.

More Inspiration on Self-Love

"I can live for two weeks on a good compliment." — Mark Twain

"The greatest thing in the world is to know how to belong to oneself." — Montaigne

"If you can't love yourself, how the hell you gonna love someone else?" — Ru Paul

"everything necessary to live a vivid life already exists in me / I am complete simply because I am imperfect" — Rupi Kaur

"The truth is that you already are what you are seeking." — Adyashanti

"I don't trust people who don't love themselves and tell me, 'I love you.' ... There is an African saying which is: Be careful when a naked person offers you a shirt." — Maya Angelou

- ♪ *Love Like This* — RY X
- ♪ *Lovesong from the Mountains* — Deuter
- ♪ *I am Light* — India.Arie

Notes

VII. SELF-DISCOVERY

"Knowing yourself is the beginning of all wisdom."

— Aristotle

Self-discovery is an endless journey within ourselves. With no true destinations, we must embrace each day and its unpredictability that shapes who we are. Through yoga, we all have the liberty to explore our distinctive character and endless capabilities by practicing themes relating to self-discovery.

This chapter presents six essential yoga class themes and inspiration relating to self-discovery: Curiosity, Heart-Opening, Honesty, Integrity, Tuning-In, and Wisdom. The theme of *Curiosity* encourages us to be more inquisitive in order to widen our understanding of ourselves and our relationship with the world. A *Heart-Opening* theme allows us to be more accepting of the positive energy around us. The theme of *Honesty* encourages us to be authentic to ourselves and others by not hiding the truth or who we are. An *Integrity* themed class inspires us to embrace our moral character. *Tuning-in* encourages us to look within ourselves for answers and peace. Last, the theme of *Wisdom* helps us to recognize our inner-knowledge and be more cognizant of the learning opportunities that surround us. Basing classes on any of these themes encourages continued self-discovery, expansion of self-knowledge, and understanding of one's significance in the world.

These self-discovery themes include content relating to centering exercises, asanas, and inspirational resources that help to plan memorable yoga classes for modern yoga students.

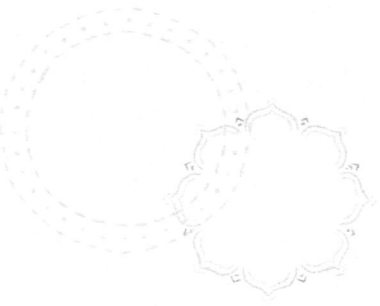

Curiosity

Curiosity is a desire to know and to have an inquisitive interest. As children, we are in a state of constant curiosity in order to learn about the world around us. Whereas, as adults, we sometimes need extra inspiration and effort to learn.

Yoga can be used as an instrument for exploring our innate curiosity through movement, breath, and meditation. These practices encourage a curious mind that desires exploration anc wisdom. As such, a curiosity-themed yoga class encourages a childlike mindset whereby the world can be considered through a new lens and perspective—fueling our sense of wonder and finding a new appreciation for our lives and the universe.

Curiosity as an Intention

Encourage students to adopt a more curious mindset. Ask them what they are curious about and would like to dedicate time and energy towards exploring. This could relate to any unanswered questions, unknown family history, something familiar that is not well understood, or a place that has never been visited. Have students set an intention to be more curious, and encourage students to maintain an inquisitive and playful mindset throughout the practice to fuel this intention.

Centering for Curiosity

Have students take *Hakini Mudra* (Problem Solving Gesture), which is said to boost brain power, intellectual capacity, memory, problem-solving, and concentration. In turn, these qualities benefit and encourage a curious mind. This mudra is also said to harmonize the left and right hemispheres of the brain.

> Take Hakini Mudra with both hands, beginning in a prayer position and spreading the fingers apart while maintaining contact at the fingertips. Then, widen the distance between the palms by a few inches. The hands should make a pyramid-

like shape. While maintaining the mudra's shape, you might also choose to tap the fingertips together in a repetitive motion, gaze at the third eye, or raise the mudra to your heart or third eye if those areas inspire more focus and balance.

While maintaining the mudra, students can repeat affirmations, such as the following:

I am a curious being; I continue to ask questions; I continue to explore; I choose to learn every day; etc.

Furthermore, lead students in a curiosity-driven sensory awareness meditation, noticing the sounds and smells around them. Have them tune in on something they might not have noticed before the meditation. Ask students to silently consider what they are learning through curiosity and how they find that inspirational, enlightening, or fun.

Curiosity through Movement

The theme of curiosity encourages us to play while challenging our perspective. An example of how to do this by playing with standing poses. In particular, students can be led into *Warrior Three* (Virabhadrasana III) before playing with *Standing Split* (Urdhva Prasarita Eka Padasana) and *Half Moon Pose* (Ardha Chandrasana) variations—including *Half Moon Twists* (Parivrtta Ardha Chandrasana) and grabbing the raised foot with the opposite hand. Offer students the option to use blocks. Further, guide students through creative transitions between these asanas and have them pay special attention to how their bodies represent creative expression.

By exploring these asanas, we are also considering how our minds and bodies react from different perspectives and in poses that challenge us in various ways. In turn, these poses help us learn new things about how our bodies can move and how we experience the benefits of the poses after safely releasing, exiting, and transitioning into counterposes.

SELF-DISCOVERY

More Inspiration on Curiosity

"The most beautiful experience we can have is the mysterious. It is the fundamental emotion that stands at the cradle of true art and true science." – Albert Einstein

"Smart people are the ones who ask the most thoughtful questions, as opposed to thinking they have all the answers. Great questions are a much better indicator of future success than great answers." – Ray Dulio

"Successful people ask better questions, and as a result, they get better answers." – Tony Robbins

"The important thing is not to stop questioning. Curiosity has its own reason for existence. One cannot help but be in awe when he contemplates the mysteries of eternity, of life, of the marvelous structure of reality. It is enough if one tries merely to comprehend a little of this mystery each day." – Albert Einstein

"Remember to look up at the stars and not down at your feet. Try to make sense of what you see and wonder about what makes the universe exist. Be curious. And however difficult life may seem, there is always something you can do and succeed at. It matters that you don't just give up." — Stephen Hawking

- ♪ *Wander* – Sarah Watson
- ♪ *The Hedgehog* – Goetz Oestlind
- ♪ *Inquisitiveness* – Beau Project
- ♪ *In the Midst of It All* – Tom Misch, Sam Wills

YOGA THEMES FOR MODERN YOGIS

Notes

Heart-Opening

To open our hearts means to be available to give and receive love, kindness, and generosity. Opening our hearts also involves being honest about how we feel and not being ashamed to make ourselves vulnerable. By practicing these qualities, we can more easily receive positive energy around us and share our joy with others.

Yoga helps to create an optimistic atmosphere that makes us more comfortable to be loving and honest with ourselves and others. During a heart-opening themed yoga class, consider the heart space as a guide for opening up emotionally and physically, as students find more spaciousness across the chest.

Heart Opening as an Intention

Have students consider how they would like to make more space in their lives. This might relate to clearing clutter, making more time for themselves, or taking up more physical space as a way to honor themselves. Then, have students set an intention to open their hearts in any general or specific ways. This heart-opening intention can also be offered to someone else.

Centering for Heart-Opening

Have students take *Pralamba Mudra* (Spreading Offerings Gesture), which is said to open the heart and calm the spirit. It also encourages feelings of devotion and compassion, in addition to releasing anxiety and ego.

> To enter the mudra, connect both hands at the thumbs and make a goal-post shape between the hands, keeping the other fingers tight together.

Ask students to repeat heart-opening affirmations, such as the following:

My heart is open; I follow my heart and reflect on my inner feelings; I listen to what my heart tells me; I open my heart to receive positive energy and joy; etc.

For a pranayama technique, have students practice diaphragmatic belly breathing. By focusing on puffing out the belly on the inhales and sucking in the belly on the exhales, space is maximized within the rib cage to feel more open across the chest. Belly breath is also important to review because it is helpful for breathing during deep chest openers when movement in the ribcage is restricted.

Heart-Opening Poses

Deep heart-opening asanas release emotional and physical tension from the chest area. They also maximize physical space within the ribcage and improve spinal flexibility that helps us to remain healthy and maintain good posture. These poses likewise symbolize the heart and the self-love that yoga embodies.

These deep heart-opening poses include *Camel Pose* (Ustrasana), *Locust Pose* (Salabhasana), Bow Pose (Dhanurasana), and *Fish Pose* (Matsyasana). Other heart-space opening options include *Cow Tilts* (Chakravakasana), *Upward-Facing Dog* (Urdhva Mukha Svanasana), and *Dancer Pose* (Natarajasana). Allow students to breathe deeply to open their hearts higher and wider into the infinite space around them. Also, reinforce the importance of engaging the core to protect the lumbar spine, and have students try to articulate every vertebra to awaken the thoracic spine that supports the ribcage and heart space.

More Heart-Opening Inspiration

"The best and most beautiful things in the world cannot be seen or even touched—they must be felt with the heart." — Helen Keller

"Only when there is purity in the heart; a heart peaceful and free from egoism--the 'I' and the 'mine.' Purity of heart and equanimity of mind are the very essence of Yoga." — Swami Satchidananda

"It all has to come from the inside." — Jimmy Hendrix

"Nobody has ever measured, not even poets, how much the heart can hold." — Zelda Fitzgerald

"Remember that wherever your heart is, there you will find your treasure." — Paulo Coelho

"Music acts like a magic key, to which the most tightly closed heart opens." — Maria Augusta von Trapp

- ♪ *Open Me Slowly* — Rena Jones
- ♪ *Space* — Siv Jakobsen
- ♪ *Light of Love* — Jai-Jagdeesh

Notes

Honesty

Honesty is to be sincere, fair, authentic, and straightforward. It also means to tell the truth and be considerate when news is difficult to share. Honesty is also necessary in order to show respect and experience peace. Honesty requires that we are also true to ourselves and our individual beliefs. Honesty brings clarity into our lives and helps us to make wise and informed decisions—especially when these are difficult or life-changing.

Honesty also relates to the yogic concept of *Satya*, which is defined as overall truthfulness, to ourselves and others. Satya considers that even the smallest white lies can create bad habits, hurt others, and lead us down an undesirable path for ourselves. Yet, these can be avoided by practicing honesty on a daily basis. Satya also respects how our lives have their own truths that differ from truths in the lives of others.

A yoga class theme surrounding honesty is a modern interpretation of Satya, which embodies truthfulness as it relates to oneself and others. Thus, a yoga class on honesty allows modern yoga students to grasp this foundational element of yoga in practical terms.

Honesty as an Intention

Have students consider a time when they were dishonest to somebody else and how that made them feel. Then, have them try the more difficult task of reflecting on when they were dishonest to themselves and how these feelings have a more profound significance. You might give examples such as making a poor decision for oneself, depriving oneself of opportunities, or undermining their full potential and earned respect. As such, have students dedicate their intention to becoming more honest with others or themselves.

Honesty Through Centering

Take *Vishuddha Mudra* (Throat Chakra Gesture) for honest communication, positive expression, and a better understanding of others. It is also said to improve listening skills.

> To take this mudra, bring both hands together with the palms facing down and loosely interweave the fingers before connecting the index fingers with the opposite thumbs to create two interlocking circles.

Have students repeat affirmations to reinforce the theme of honesty, such as the following:

> *I am honest to myself and others; honesty relieves stress from my life; I speak the truth to myself and others*; etc.

For another centering technique, guide students in a simple breathing exercise by exhaling feelings of dishonesty and inhaling acceptance of the truth. Repeat this for several rounds before having students pause and note any feelings of emotional release. Then, draw their attention to any physical release experienced in their throat, chest, and shoulders.

Honesty Through Poses

To represent honesty, incorporate throat-opening positions, such as *Extended Puppy Pose* (Uttana Shishosana) variations and *Camel Pose* (Ustrasana) variations. These asanas can release stress across the chest and encourage open communication.

Thread the Needle Pose (Parsva Balasana) also represents honesty by releasing tightness held across the shoulders and forearms, while opening up one side of the chest at a time. Students can deepen the heart opener with control by exploring the options of lifting the forward hand to the sky or taking a half bind. This asana allows students to be honest with themselves by taking a variation that is kind to their bodies and to release and breathe healing energy into any stagnant tension that might hold them back from being honest with others.

Encourage students to be honest to themselves by also incorporating props for challenging or relaxing positions when they might wish to have a little extra support or the opportunity to experience a deeper expression of a pose. For example, *Child's Pose* (Balasana) can be taken while elevating the elbows onto blocks, which intensifies a stretch along the forearms and back muscles. By contrast, Child's Pose can be taken while sitting on a block or blanket, which can make the pose more restful and accessible to some students. The use of props, such as in these instances, represents honesty because they require listening to the body to make student-specific adjustments.

More Inspiration on Honesty

"The real things haven't changed. It is still best to be honest and truthful; to make the most of what we have; to be happy with simple pleasures; and have courage when things go wrong." – Laura Ingalls Wilder

"Be yourself; everyone else is already taken." – Oscar Wilde

"Never be afraid to raise your voice for honesty and truth and compassion against injustice and lying and greed. If people all over the world...would do this, it would change the earth." – William Faulkner

"If you do not tell the truth about yourself, you cannot tell it about other people." – Virginia Woolf

"To believe in something, and not to live it, is dishonest." – Mahatma Gandhi

"Honesty is the first chapter of the book of wisdom." – Thomas Jefferson

- ♪ *Honesty* – Thrupence
- ♪ *Truth* – Andri Hart
- ♪ *Satya (Truthfulness)* – Michael Mandrell and Benjy Wertheimer
- ♪ *Throat Chakra* – Beautiful Chorus

SELF-DISCOVERY

Notes

Integrity

Integrity means to be honest and to have strong moral principles. It also means that one follows their own values and is respectful towards others. Integrity honors our unique and expressive characteristics and embraces who we are. Thus, integrity in yoga practice requires that we make the practice our own.

Integrity is representative of the yogic philosophy idea of *Asteya*, meaning non-stealing and non-greediness, and it can include actions, speech, and thoughts. In reference to Asteya, Gandhi said, "The need to steal essentially arises because of a lack of faith in ourselves to be able to create what we need by ourselves." In this regard, yoga encourages non-stealing, which encourages us to also practice integrity by being true to ourselves and honoring what we already have.

Integrity as an Intention

Have students consider a moral principle that they would like to make stronger, or reflect on circumstances when they could have acted with greater integrity—such as a dishonest interaction with someone or something that they had done in secret. Have students mark this as a moment from which they can move forward with greater integrity, and encourage them to dedicate their practice towards forgiving themselves and tapping into the kindness and honor within themselves.

Centering with Integrity

Practice *Anjali Mudra* (My Essence Meets Your Essence) with palms together at the heart center, representing respect toward self and the universe—essential elements of integrity. It is also said to enhance compassion, generosity, and gratitude.

> Take Anjali mudra with palms together in prayer at the heart center, representing respect toward oneself and the universe. This mudra shape also symbolizes how

an affirmation can be placed like a seed between the palms and guided toward our hearts as a symbol of respect, humility, and integrity.

While holding Anjali Mudra, have students repeat integrity-inspired affirmations, such as the following:

I am genuine; I am honest; I practice non-stealing in every sense; I live my life with integrity; etc.

Furthermore, have students try breathing with purpose and fully expanding the lungs and belly with deep breaths in their own time. This reinforces the idea of integrity by allowing the breath to inflate the body with honor and respect.

Poses for Integrity

Standing poses have a particular significance for an integrity-themed practice. They reinforce our ability to feel grounded and they represent the idea of believing in ourselves by taking a stand on matters relating to integrity and self-respect.

Mountain Pose (Tadasana) is the foundation for all standing positions because it involves finding equilibrium and strength in a simple stance. Tadasana also represents the integrity of an unmoving mountain.

The concept of integrity can also be challenged by playing with *Chair Pose* (Utkatasana) and its variations—including twists on each side, or coming onto the toes while rising and carefully lowering towards the earth again. Students can also try balancing on the ball of one foot while they extend the other and sit lower onto the heel. Focus on the integrity of level hips and an evenly engaged core and thighs.

Furthermore, single standing leg balances can also be explored, including Tree Pose, Eagle Pose (Garudasana), and Extended Hand-to-Big-Toe Pose (Utthita Hasta Padangustasana). These poses can challenge us to keep the hips level and body still to feel the full integrity of the poses.

More Inspiration on Integrity

"Peace of mind comes when we exercise our right to be honest, especially with ourselves." – Jack R. Rose

"Being honest may not get you a lot of friends but it'll always get you the right ones." – John Lennon

"The greatness of a man is not in how much wealth he acquires, but in his integrity and his ability to affect those around him positively." – Bob Marley

"Waste no more time arguing about what a good man should be. Be one." – Marcus Aurelius

"Integrity is doing the right thing, even when no one is watching." – C.S. Lewis

- ♪ *Integrity* – Shimmer
- ♪ *Asteya* – Baird Hersey & Prana
- ♪ *Ethics* – Syndrome

Notes

Tuning-in

Tuning-in is a mindfulness and self-discovery technique that involves looking inward for answers. This is an important practice because we can otherwise develop an unaccommodating perspective when we become comfortable with a set routine, lifestyle, or bias. We might unknowingly become trapped by our own boundaries, become more easily stressed, and overthink or overlook important elements in our lives.

Instead of feeling restricted, we must step back and tune into our authentic selves and emotions by looking within ourselves for guidance. This practice can help us think optimally when making decisions or considering issues through a new perspective—thereby, discovering focus and balance within.

The concept of tuning-in also relates to the third eye chakra. This chakra is located between our eyebrows and represents insight, wisdom, and intellect. It also represents a way to see our world without our traditional sense of sight.

Tuning-In as an Intention

Have students' intentions surround the concept of tuning-in and our third eye—to look within ourselves for guidance and clarity. Tap into this mindset by having them consider how they might sometimes restrict their outlook or ability to make decisions that are authentic to themselves. Examples include following directions when answers are within, following a routine when self-inspired change is needed, or listening to the opinions of others rather than one's capable thoughts.

With hands in a prayer position at the heart, have students dedicate the practice towards strengthening their ability to look inward for answers and guidance. Seal the intention by raising the hands to the forehead with thumbs pressed firmly on the third eye—connecting the heart and mind while looking inward.

Centering for Tuning-In

Begin with a simple meditation that focuses on deep and even breaths. Have students notice any new sensations in their bodies and breathe into them. Have them also acknowledge thoughts before sending them away. Encourage them to focus on the present moment within themselves.

Then, in any comfortable position, have students continue centering by repeat affirmations for tuning-in, such as the following:

> *All the answers I need I see within me; I trust my intuition; I respect my inner teacher; I see all things with clarity*; etc.

For an alternative meditation, try the *Looking Within* exercise with *Shanmukhi Mudra* (Tuning into Silence Gesture). This helps to bring the mind inward and become more contemplative

> This involves sitting in *Lotus Pose* (Padmasana) or another comfortable seat while cupping all fingertips over the eyes to block off outer vision and look within. For a deeper tuning-in experience, try closing off the other senses; Cover the eyelids with just the index and middle fingers, while closing the ears with the thumbs, pressing the ring fingers to cover the nostrils, the pinky fingers against the creases of closed lips.

After explaining the Looking Within exercise, tell students to take a deep breath and stay there for approximately ten to twenty seconds so they feel welcome to stay in the mudra. And ask students to take note of any new feelings that their body or mind might reveal when they tune in with restricted senses.

Poses for Tuning-In

Begin with *Warrior One* (Virabhadrasana I), while having students be mindful of every muscle activation, internal and external rotation, and alignment. Encourage students to keep their intentions in mind and have them notice how their bodies feel different during a transition from *Warrior Two* (Virabhadrasana II) into *Exalted/Reverse Warrior Pose* (Viparita Virabhadrasana). Have students open the heart and feel the vulnerability of the pose while surrendering to any emotions that occur from this transition. Then, ask them to close their eyes or maintain a soft downward gaze while finding balance within.

Moreover, most asanas can be practiced with closed eyes—representing a greater tuning-in experience. Focusing on seeing through the third eye chakra, try flowing through movements with an internal focus, or holding poses such as *Child's Pose* (Balasana) with the forehead and third eye resting on the ground.

More Inspiration for Tuning-In

"The summit of happiness is reached when a person is ready to be what he is." – Erasmus of Rotterdam

"In the midst of winter, I found there was, within me, an invincible summer. And that makes me happy. For it says that no matter how hard the world pushes against me, within me, there's something stronger – something better, pushing right back." – Albert Camus

"What lies behind us and what lies before us are tiny matters compared to what lies within us." – Ralph Waldo Emerson

"Everything in the universe is within you. Ask all from yourself." – Rumi

- ♪ *Drifting* – Sarah Watson
- ♪ *Four Senses* – East Forest
- ♪ *Call Within* (Instrumental) – Manose

YOGA THEMES FOR MODERN YOGIS

Notes

Wisdom

Wisdom means to have knowledge, experience, and noble judgment. It is not something that we are born with or can simply acquire; Rather wisdom is developed throughout our lives and it is meant to be shared.

Yoga helps us to become wiser in numerous ways. The practice is rich with antiquated and modern texts, practice styles, teachings, and lessons from gurus and practitioners. By showing up on the mat, students are already open to receiving wisdom—which can also be incorporated as a specific class theme.

Wisdom as an Intention

Have students consider what they are hoping to learn on or off of the mat. For example, this could be a pose, a language, an instrument, a concept, a particular topic, or a specific problem to solve. Then, encourage students to set an intention surrounding how they would like to continue building upon their wisdom. Have their practice guide them to continuously learn, grow, make positive decisions, and share wisdom with others.

Centering for Wisdom

Open the practice with a calm and reflective meditation using *Jnana/Gyana Mudra* on one or both hands. Jnana Mudra is commonly called the mudra of wisdom and knowledge, and it helps to keep the mind focused.

> With a downward-facing palm, extend the pinky, ring, and middle fingers, while tucking the index finger into the thumb crease.

While in Jnana Mudra, encourage students to repeat wisdom-inspired affirmations, such as the following:

> *I always seek guidance; my inner wisdom guides me; I am wise; I continue to learn; I am ready to receive wisdom; wisdom flows through me; I offer inner guidance to myself and others;* The answers I seek are within me; etc.

For another centering technique, consider leading students in a wisdom-inspired meditation by noticing things around them that they had overlooked. Then, focus on how the body naturally breathes and imagine every part of the body that helps us breathe and is affected by our breath—representing how wisdom comes from within. Treat every moment as a learning experience in and outside of the body.

Poses for Wisdom

Incorporate spinal twist variations in a wisdom-themed class because they help us learn more about the body as an interconnected being with natural imbalances. For example, take *Reclined/Supine Spinal Twists* (Supta Matsyendrasana) and its variations, including the Yin-inspired *Cat Pulling its Tail*. Have students feel the shoulders open and the knees drop to one side at a time. Encourage them to have the wisdom to notice the differences in each side of the body.

Another twisting asana option for exploring the concept of wisdom is *Seated Spinal Twist Pose* (Ardha Matsyendrasana). This pose allows students to have more control over their twist and focus on turning from the belly while raising the crown of the head skyward and drawing the shoulders back—becoming more cognizant of the body and tapping into self-knowledge.

Head-to-Knee Forward Bend (Janu Sirsasana) also offers a gentle turn of the spine and an external hip rotation as the body folds over the extended leg. This pose reminds us to bend from the hips and make adjustments that we know that our individual bodies need—such as placing a blanket under the bent knee or the knee of the extended leg. Inner wisdom will shine through.

When repeating positions on their alternate sides, ask students to consider why one side might feel different from the other. Mention how each side can be a teacher to the other, and a position can feel completely different day-to-day. Pointing this out can encourage them to discover more about themselves and what yoga means to them. As such, they are tapping into their inner wisdom and inspiring themselves to continue their never-ending learning journey.

More Wisdom Inspiration

"No one should be ashamed to admit they are wrong, which is but saying, in other words, that they are wiser today than they were yesterday." – Alexander Pope

"It takes two years to learn to speak / and sixty to learn to keep quiet." – Ernest Hemmingway

"If your mind is empty, it is always ready for anything, it is open to everything. In the beginner's mind there are many possibilities, but in the expert's mind, there are few. – Shunryu Suzuki

"Learning without reflection is a waste. Reflection without learning is dangerous." – Confucius

"The good news is that the moment you decide that what you know is more important than what you have been taught to believe, you will have shifted gears in your quest for abundance. Success comes from within, not from without." – Ralph Waldo Emerson

"For those who have an intense urge for Spirit and wisdom, it sits near them, waiting." – Patañjali

"We can know only that we know nothing. And that is the highest degree of human wisdom." – Leo Tolstoy

♪ *Wisdom* – Kazutoshi
♪ *Mind* – From Alfie

♪ *Wisdom and Compassion* – Nawang Khechog

Notes

VIII. BEYOND OURSELVES

*"A human... experiences himself... as something separated from the rest...
Our task must be to free ourselves... by widening our circle of compassion to embrace all living
creatures and the whole of nature in its beauty."*

— Albert Einstein

The earlier chapters in this book addressed themes that relate to ourselves and our place in the world. By contrast, this chapter focuses on yoga class themes that honor others. At its core, yoga is about unity and connecting with the world beyond ourselves. Thus, it is important to also consider adopting class themes and intentions that are dedicated to others.

This chapter includes eight yoga class themes that encourage us to better relate and connect with others. These also challenge us to have a more positive impact on the world and all living things. These themes are Forgiveness, Generosity, Loving-Kindness, Nature & the Earth, Peace, Relationships, Selflessness, and Understanding.

The theme of *Forgiveness* inspires us to release grudges that we might hold against others. *Generosity* encourages us to give to others without expecting anything in return. The theme of *Loving-Kindness* inspires us to be unconditionally kind and loving towards others. *Nature & the Earth* helps to strengthen our relationship with all living things. *Peace* allows us to be at ease with everyone. The theme of *Relationships* focuses on improving our ties with others. *Selflessness* encourages us to be altruistic and practice kindness. Last, the theme of *Understanding* challenges us to view the world from others' points of view.

These themes are supported by suggestions for centering techniques, asana recommendations, and inspirational material—helping modern yogis build connections beyond ourselves.

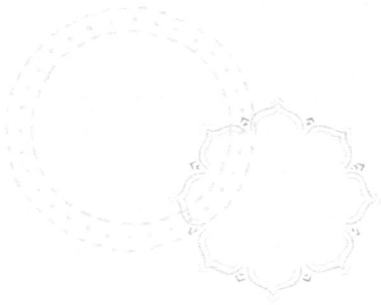

Forgiveness

Forgiveness means letting go of hostility, resentment, bitterness, anger, and desire for vengeance towards someone else or themselves based on feelings of wrongdoing. The hope is that by forgiving, we can release a burden of stress and experience peace within ourselves.

Because forgiveness is voluntary and internal, the process does not have a time frame and it can reveal itself differently to everyone. For example, someone might try to understand the point of view of the wrong-doer in order to forgive, or, they might try other techniques such as mindfulness practices or seeking advice from others. Another way to improve our ability to forgive is by practicing yoga, which encourages us to be forgiving of ourselves and release hostility that can prevent us from forgiving others.

Forgiveness as an Intention

Have students consider any resentment that they might be holding onto. For example, this could relate to a specific person or an experience. Encourage them to dedicate their practice towards dissolving resentment, either related to a specific element or in a general sense, and to set a yoga practice intention of forgiveness to experience peace.

Centering for Forgiveness

Take *Varada Mudra* (Forgiveness Gesture), which is taken as an offering of forgiveness, mercy, and good wishes.

> To take this single-handed mudra, extend all fingers together and rest the hand on the knee with the palm facing down.
>
> Alternatively, the palm can be turned away from the body with the fingertips down so that onlookers can view the mudra. In this case, Varada Mudra represents the

welcoming of others and the offering of charity, compassion, and sincerity—which are active ways to express forgiveness.

Have students repeat affirmations related to forgiveness, such as the following:

I release all hostility; I let go of all grudges; I choose to understand and forgive; I forgive others; I forgive myself; etc.

Further, have students take a meditation with a simple pranayama exercise whereby students inhale clean, positive energy through the nose, and exhale toxic negative energy through the mouth. Repeat this several times so that students can feel mental clarity and release any hostility they might have held.

Poses for Forgiveness

Have students take *Lizard Pose* (Utthan Pristhasana) with the back knee lifted from the ground before lowering the knee to the floor—noticing the sensation of letting go that is correlated to forgiveness and how we feel after forgiving or apologizing.

From this Low Lizard Pose, students can walk their hands behind them and lean back to open the chest and neck as an expression of humility, emotional release, and universal forgiveness. With the knee to the ground, students can also reach behind to grab the foot and draw it towards them for a deeper stretch. Have them release the leg carefully again and consider the difference between discomfort and comfort—representing our change in emotions after we forgive and apologize. This also exemplified how a simple change in a position can turn an active pose into a passive pose, symbolizing how we can take simple measures to release grudges and resolve issues with others and ourselves.

More Forgiveness Inspiration

"We must develop and maintain the capacity to forgive. He who is devoid of the power to forgive is devoid of the power to love." — Martin Luther King

"Any fool can criticize, complain, and condemn—and most fools do. But it takes character and self-control to be understanding and forgiving." — Dale Carnegie

"The weak can never forgive / Forgiveness is the attribute of the strong." — Mahatma Gandhi

"Today I decided to forgive you. Not because you apologized or because you acknowledged the pain that you caused me, but because my soul deserves peace." — Najwa Zebian

"Apologies aren't meant to change the past; they are meant to change the future." — Kevin Hancock

"Never ruin an apology with an excuse." — Benjamin Franklin

"The best revenge is not to be like your enemy." — Marcus Aurelius

- ♪ *Forgiveness* — Sarah McLachlan
- ♪ *Baby Can I Hold You* — Tracy Chapman
- ♪ *Let Go* — Chama Wijnen

YOGA THEMES FOR MODERN YOGIS

Notes

Generosity

Generosity is about giving to others, helping those less fortunate, and contributing without expecting anything in return. Generosity is important for living in a kind and supportive community. And while generosity is a trait that intends to help others, it also brings joy and fulfillment to the person who gives.

Generosity is a significant philosophical element of yoga and relates to the ancient concept of *Aparigraha*, which means non-attachment and non-possessiveness in Sanskrit. It is the belief that more than enough resources exist for everyone in the world and that we can all afford to be generous. Thus, generosity allows us to experience a deeper appreciation of yoga and its principles beyond the asana practice. Further, practicing generosity-themed yoga classes can inspire students to tap into their inherent kindness and feel newfound warmth in their lives through giving.

Generosity as an Intention

Have students consider how they can be more generous. This could be abstract, such as showing more small acts of kindness, being a better listener, or helping those less fortunate. Or, students could consider something more specific, such as doing a particular favor to someone they know. Then, encourage them to dedicate their practice towards nurturing their inner-generosity and adopting their intentions into their daily routine.

Generosity Centering

Take *Vyapak Anjali/Pushpaputa Mudra* (All-Pervading Offerings Gesture), which encourages honesty, compassion, and generosity towards the self and others. It also helps to appreciate the universe, create inner-spaciousness, and spread positivity.

> To practice this mudra, open both palms and hold them together along the outer sides of the pinky fingers and palms as if to give or receive an offering.

Holding the mudra, have students repeat affirmations for generosity, such as the following:

I am generous and kind; I make a difference in my community; I share positivity with others; I release possessiveness; I have more than I need; Contributing brings me joy; etc.

As a meditation and pranayama exercise, have students imagine breathing in abundance, and exhaling generosity. Repeat this for several rounds to encourage contentment and the desire to give.

Poses for Generosity

Have students take *Goddess Pose* (Utkata Konasana) and *Garland Pose/Yogi Squat* (Malasana) because these asanas represent our ability to open up and share with others. In particular, these poses symbolize giving one's heart and spirit to those around us while feeling the warmth of generosity that is received from the world. These asanas are also hip and chest opening positions also represent how we can outwardly share positive energy with others and be more generous in our everyday lives.

Furthermore, have students rest the back of their palms to the ground during Corpse Pose (Savasana) to close the practice with open hands and an open heart to the sky. Students might choose to raise the heart even higher by laying on a bolster or blanket and allowing the shoulders to release. After finding a suitable position, allow students to imagine sharing positive energy with others within the practice space.

More Generosity Inspiration

"The secret to living is giving." – Tony Robbins

"You give but little when you give of your possessions. It is when you give of yourself that you truly give." – Khalil Gibran

"Give what you have. To someone, it may be better than you dare to think." – Henry Wadsworth Longfellow

"The more we genuinely care about others, the greater our own happiness and inner peace." – Allan Lokos

"Give a bowl of rice to a man and you will feed him for a day. Teach him how to grow his own rice and you will save his life." – Confucius

"A generous heart, kind speech, and a life of service and compassion are the things which renew humanity." – Gautama Buddha

"Generosity is the most natural outward expression of an inner attitude of compassion and loving-kindness." – Dalai Lama XIV

- ♪ *Generosity* – Gogenheim
- ♪ *Aparigraha* – Baird Hersey & Prana
- ♪ *People Help the People* – Birdy
- ♪ *Offering* – Peter Kater, R. Carlos Nakai

YOGA THEMES FOR MODERN YOGIS

Notes

Loving-Kindness

Loving-kindness involves spreading joy, compassion, and equanimity for all beings, which is achieved through unconditional love and kindness. It requires getting rid of preconceived notions of others and simply recognizing what unites us.

Practicing a theme of loving-kindness in yoga is a positive reminder to be respectful, generous, and loving to others and ourselves. This timeless theme also encapsulates the yogic concept of *Maitri*, which is defined as friendliness and loving-kindness. This style of practice also overlaps with a *meta/metta* practice, which is about becoming one's own friend and being better equipped to love others.

Loving-Kindness as an Intention

Encourage students to enter a general mindset of unconditional friendliness, kindness, respect, and love. Allow them to imagine giving and receiving love. Then, ask students to either choose to set a general intention to fuel a mindset of loving-kindness, or to share loving-kindness with someone specific or a particular group of people or living things. Note that if students would prefer a meta practice, they can dedicate a loving-kindness practice to themselves.

Centering for Loving-Kindness

Take *Hridaya Mudra* (Compassionate Heart Gesture), which represents unconditional love, genuine affection, empathy, compassion, and communication. This mudra also helps to strengthen the heart and release trapped emotions and stress, reduce anxiety, and lower the heart rate.

> To take this one-handed mudra, curl the index finger into the crease of the thumb while pinching together the points of the thumb, middle, and ring fingers, and extending the pinky finger.

Have students repeat affirmations for loving-kindness, such as the following:

May you be safe; May you be happy; May you be healthy; May you live a life at ease; etc.

This affirmation may be repeated a few times with different dedications: once for oneself, once for a loved one, once for another living thing, once for a stranger, and once for someone who has caused disagreement.

Furthermore, guide students in a loving-kindness meditation by having them imagine someone who loves them—whether that is a family member or companion, for example. Have them consider how that love makes them feel. Then, have students wish those feelings upon someone else. Have students also wish those feelings on everyone around them and imagine that those people do the same. Extend this loving-kindness to all living things. Ultimately, have students imagine the entire universe experiencing loving-kindness. This visualization exercise helps to create a blissful and generous mood to set the tone for a loving-kindness-themed class.

Poses for Loving-Kindness

Loving-kindness is represented by holding gentle chest openers, such as *Sphinx Pose* (Salamba Bhujangasana) and Seal Pose. These poses release the heart and allow positivity to disperse within the practice space and beyond—sharing loving-kindness.

For a deeper chest opener, consider incorporating *Bridge Pose* (Setu Bandha Sarvangasana), lifting the heart to the sky, while representing a bridge of loving-kindness between ourselves and others. To make the pose more relaxing and to feel a deeper release across the chest, students can take a *supported* Bridge Pose by propping their hips and sacrum onto a block.

Another asana for loving-kindness is Fish Pose (Matsyasana), which lifts the heart to the sky and above the rest of the body—signifying the importance of tuning in to the heart and finding relaxation through an open heart and finding relaxation through an open chest.

More Inspiration on Loving-Kindness

"It is good to love many things, for therein lies the true strength, and whosoever loves much performs much, and can accomplish much, and what is done in love is well done." – Vincent Van Gogh

"Not all of us can do great things. But we can do small things with great love." – Mother Teresa

"I've learned that people will forget what you said, people will forget what you did, but people will never forget how you made them feel." – Maya Angelou

"A drop of love is more than an ocean of intellect." – Blaise Pascal

"Kindness in words creates confidence. / Kindness in thinking creates profoundness. / Kindness in giving creates love." – Lao Tzu

"All love is expansion; all selfishness is contraction. Love is therefore the only law of life. He who loves lives, he who is selfish is dying. Therefore, love for love's sake, because it is the only law of life, just as you breathe to live." – Swami Vivekananda

"Do not be content with showing friendship in words alone, let your heart burn with loving kindness for all who may cross your path." – Bahá'u'lláh

"The first element of true love is loving kindness. The essence of loving kindness is being able to offer happiness. You can be the sunshine for another person. You can't offer happiness until you have it for yourself. So build a home inside by accepting yourself and learning to love and heal yourself. Learn how to practice mindfulness in such a way that you can create moments of happiness and joy for your own nourishment. Then you have something to offer the other person." – Thich Nhat Hanh

- ♪ *Loving-Kindness* – Vimassana
- ♪ *In Her Heart* – Jonas Oskar
- ♪ *I'll Keep You Safe* – sagun

YOGA THEMES FOR MODERN YOGIS

Notes

Nature & the Earth

Nature refers to the natural elements of earth, including wild landscapes, oceans, creatures, trees, flowers, and natural formations. It is the untouched parts of the world that are appreciated for being what they are rather than what they can be turned into.

A modern yoga class theme of nature and the earth helps us to appreciate the beauty of the natural world that surrounds us. It also helps to expand our mindset beyond our man-made surroundings and to be compassionate towards all living things. This theme also represents universal love and considers the legacy and footprint that we leave behind. This theme can also help to put us back in touch with the natural world that can be taken for granted in this modern age.

Nature as an Intention

Encourage students to consider their impact on the earth and how they can better connect with nature. This could be as simple as appreciating more time outside, being less wasteful, etc. Then, have students set an intention to be more in tune with their natural surroundings and the beauty of the earth.

Centering for the Earth

Take *Prithivi Mudra* (Earth Gesture), which pays homage to the ground and natural energy around us while detaching from ourselves. This mudra connects us to the earth, which provides the foundation from which we also gain stability.

> To take this mudra, extend the right hand and fingers outward and away from the body, while pinching the tips of the thumb and ring finger together.

Holding Prithivi Mudra, have students repeat earth and nature-inspired affirmations, such as the following:

I am connected to all life; I appreciate nature's rugged beauty; I respect the earth; We are all connected: every person, creature, and living thing; etc.

Furthermore, lead students in a *nature meditation*. Have them consider how they feel when they breathe in fresh air, listen to birds chirping, walk under towering trees, feel sand in their toes, and admire streams, lakes, and powerful oceans. They might take a mental trip to an outdoor place that they love, or they might connect with the nature already around them or nearby. Ask them whether they feel at ease and are happy as they become joined with nature. Have them maintain that feeling throughout the practice.

Also, make sure to review *Ujjayi* Pranayama, which imitates the sound of ocean waves. Have students imagine they are on an empty beach with waves rolling in on the inhale and waves breaking on the exhales. Have them take note of the calmness they feel. Have them revisit these relaxing waves at any point during the practice.

Poses for Connecting to the Earth & Nature

Most yoga poses are named after the earth and various elements of nature, such as plants, animals, and natural phenomena. Underscore the significance behind the names of these poses throughout the class in order to reinforce the connection between yoga, nature, and ourselves.

For example, explain how poses allow us to experience the perspectives of other living beings, such as how we can slither like a snake in *Cobra Pose* (Bhujangasana), or stretch like a dog in *Upward-Facing Dog* (Urdhva Mukha Svanasana) and *Downward-Facing Dog* (Adho Mukha Svanasana). You might also incorporate *Tree Pose* (Vrksasana) and its variations, which embody our deep-rooted connection to our wild and beautiful earth. Ask students to extend their arms like branches and their fingers like leaves.

Furthermore, remind students to salute the sun every time they reach into *Upward Salute* (Urdhva Hastasana) during a *Sun Salutation*

(Surya Namaskar)—recognizing and appreciating the sun that gives life, warmth, and light to the world.

More Nature & Earth Inspiration

"Cherish sunsets, wild creatures and wild places. Have a love affair with the wonder and beauty of the earth." — Stewart Udall

"If you truly love nature, you will find beauty everywhere." — Vincent Van Gogh

"Nature reminds us what it means to be human." — Terry Tempest Williams

"Time and again we go out two together under the old trees, lie down again between the flowers, face to face with the sky." — Rilke

"Be like the sun for grace and mercy. Be like the night to cover others' faults. Be like running water for generosity. Be like death for rage and anger. Be like the Earth for modesty. Appear as you are. Be as you appear." — Rumi

"Live in each season as it passes; breathe the air, drink the drink, taste the fruit, and resign yourself to the influence of the earth." — Henry David Thoreau

- ♪ *Grounded* — East Forest
- ♪ *Wild Mountain Thyme* — Stephen Wake
- ♪ *In the Middle of Nature* — Calm Music Zone
- ♪ *Nature Calling* — Somaya Kudri

YOGA THEMES FOR MODERN YOGIS

Notes

Peace

Peace is a state of equality and tranquility that is experienced among beings or within the self. It is a harmonious existence, and it requires being at ease and accepting of others and ourselves. These feelings of peace can be practiced in yoga by coming to terms with ourselves, respecting others, and finding a state of calm.

Overall, yoga is a peaceful practice. It encourages us to be at peace with ourselves, experience a more peaceful mindset, and experience harmony with all beings through unconditional respect. Thus, peace is an important yoga class theme for modern yogis. In particular, peace in contemporary yoga can be practiced by practicing tranquility through meditation, calmness in poses, self-respect, and mindfulness of others.

Peace as an Intention

Allow students to consider how they would like to experience more peace. For example, this could be peace between them and someone else, peace within themselves, or peace that they wish upon others. Allow this desire for harmony to shape their intentions for sharing and experiencing peace. Allow this positivity to guide their yoga practice and find greater peace in their daily lives.

Centering for Peace

Have students take *Shukri Mudra* (Gesture for Virtuous Action & Purity), which helps to enter a peaceful state of mind. This mudra is also said to calm the nerves and boost immunity.

> To enter this mudra, extend the arms outward and away from the body. Then, pinch all five fingers together on each hand.

While in Shukri Mudra, ask students to repeat affirmations for peace, such as the following:

I am at peace; I find tranquility within myself; I accept everyone; I wish peace upon others; All is calm and well; etc.

For additional centering, lead students in a simple breathing exercise by inhaling peace and exhaling tension and negative feelings. Repeat this for several rounds before pausing and having students consider the peacefulness that surrounds them and is within them.

Poses for Peace

Peace is represented by *Warrior* (Virabhadrasana) poses. These positions symbolize honor and the choice to act peacefully despite having the strength to fight. Warriors also represent people coming together for a shared cause. Moreover, warrior-inspired poses can be practiced in unison with other yogis—representing a group of diverse warriors at peace with one another.

In particular, transitioning from *Warrior One* (Virabhadrasana I) to *Humble Warrior* (Baddha Virabhadrasana) represents a devoted warrior's bow of respect. Another option is taking *Peaceful Warrior* (Shanti Virabhadrasana), which helps to open the heart to oneself and to others. These simple yet deeply significant gestures are powered by inner strength and universal peace within oneself.

Furthermore, have students take *Extended Hand-to-Big-Toe Pose* (Utthita Hasta Padangustasana) and bow over the lifted leg—representing peace and humility towards oneself and others. This balancing pose also requires stillness, which signifies the importance of experiencing peace during asana practice.

Additionally, *Hero Pose* (Virasana) offers a peaceful seat to tune in and find a sense of calm. It also represents a hero that helps others and radiates peace to those around them.

More Inspiration on Peace

"Peace and joy happen neither in the quietness of the accomplishments of the marketplace, but only from within." — Sadhguru

"The life of inner peace, being harmonious and without stress, is the easiest type of existence." — Norman Vincent Peale

"Do not let the behavior of others destroy your inner peace." — Dalai Lama

"When the power of love overcomes the love of power, the world will know peace." — Mahatma Gandhi

"Peace cannot be kept by force; it can only be achieved by understanding." — Albert Einstein

"If we have no peace, it is because we have forgotten that we belong to each other." — Mother Teresa

"You may say I'm a dreamer, but I'm not the only one. I hope someday you'll join us. And the world will live as one." — John Lennon

- ♪ *Shanti (Peace Out)* — MC YOGI
- ♪ *Dance of Ganesha* — Ajeet
- ♪ *Imagine* — Jack Johnson
- ♪ *Peace* — Johann Eder

YOGA THEMES FOR MODERN YOGIS

Notes

Relationships

Relationships describe our acquaintance and connection to others. These can include our relationships with family, friends, co-workers, strangers, and ourselves. Thus, relationships can be strong and represented by lasting bonds, or they can be less significant.

Yoga can be used as an instrument for fostering healthy and lasting relationships. Not only can it help us to learn more about ourselves, but it can also encourage us to respect and love others. It can also inspire us to respect others to the same or greater extent that they respect us. Thus, relationships make a timeless yoga class theme.

Relationships as an Intention

Have students reflect on an important relationship in their life. Have them consider what has strengthened their bond and what that relationship means to them. Have them consider the sense of belonging and importance that they feel.

As a practice intention, encourage students to wish those feelings of a meaningful relationship upon another—whether that is a loved one, a stranger, or themselves. They might even choose a group of people or someone that they wish to build a stronger relationship with. Or, they could choose an intention to improve their relationship with themselves.

Centering for Relationships

Have students take *Shikhara Mudra* (Peak of the Mountain), which can represent the spiritual presence of love and friendship, in addition to acknowledging family and friends.

> To enter this mudra with one or both hands, simply make a thumbs-up gesture. As such, each hand will be in a light fist with the thumbs extended and pointing upwards.

Holding the mudra, consider having students repeat affirmations to be more mindful and appreciative of others. These can include the following:

> *I strengthen relationships every day; I am grateful for my friends and family; I open up to others; I respect my relationship with myself; I wish everyone love;* etc.

As a simple meditation, have students inhale pure positivity, and on their exhales, have them send that energy towards their loved ones and anyone they have dedicated their practice to. Have them notice a deeper connection with others that comes from within.

Relationships Through Poses

Pyramid Pose (Parsvottanasana) symbolizes friendship because of its solid and supportive base that represents a strong relationship. The asana also represents the symbolic structures that humans have built together throughout history and illustrates how we are all greater when we support one another.

A class surrounding relationships might also explore a family of poses, such as underscoring the relationship between different *Warrior* (Virabhadrasana) variations. Highlighting the similarities and differences between poses in the same asana family illustrates how modern asana practice has evolved through relationships between poses—and that we can also build a unique relationship with yoga.

More Inspiration on Relationships

"The way to develop the best that is in a person is by appreciation and encouragement."
– Charles Schwab

"No man is a failure who has friends." – Philip van Doren Stern

BEYOND OURSELVES

"A friend is someone who knows all about you and still loves you." – Elbert Hubbard

"Once I knew only darkness and stillness... my life was without past or future... but a little word from the fingers of another fell into my hand that clutched at emptiness, and my heart leaped to the rapture of living." – Helen Keller

"To the world you may be just one person but to one person you may be the world." – Brandi Snyder

"Close friends are truly life's treasures. Sometimes they know us better than we know ourselves. With gentle honesty, they are there to guide and support us, to share our laughter and our tears. Their presence reminds us that we are never really alone." – Vincent van Gogh

"Our fingerprints don't fade from the lives we've touched." – Robert Pattinson

"...love your crooked neighbour. With your crooked heart." – W.H. Auden

- ♪ *In This Together* – Boil The Ocean
- ♪ *Stand by Me* – Tracy Chapman
- ♪ *Open* – Rhye
- ♪ *Better Together* – Jack Johnson
- ♪ *Our House* – Ed Patrick

Notes

Selflessness

Selflessness means to put others before ourselves. It requires us to be more concerned with the needs and desires of others, to be unselfish and altruistic, and to strive to give more than we receive. Selflessness can include acts of goodwill, compassion, devotion, and kindness without wanting or expecting anything in return.

Selflessness also represents the practice of Karma Yoga, which says that we can purify our hearts and improve the world by serving others—a practice beyond poses, pranayama, and meditation. Thus, selflessness shares many of its foundational qualities with yoga.

Selflessness as an Intention

Have students consider how they can be less concerned with themselves and be more selfless. For example, this could relate to tiny gestures or larger offerings. Have them consider who they might be able to help, and encourage students to dedicate their practice to them. Students could select someone else, a group of people, or another living thing. Allow their selected intention and the theme of selflessness to guide their practice.

Centering for Selflessness

Take *Varada Mudra* (Wish Fulfilling Gesture), which is a mudra for giving, compassion, and sincerity—important qualities for practicing selflessness.

> To take this single-handed mudra, extend all fingers together and point them down with the palm facing away from the body and towards onlookers.

> Note: Varada Mudra represents forgiveness when it is applied by resting the inner palm onto the leg and allowing the mudra to face inwards.

Another centering technique for fostering selflessness can involve repeating theme-specific affirmations, such as the following:

> *We all deserve respect, compassion, and kindness; I focus on what I can do to help others; I am selfless in nature; We all need love*; etc.

As an additional centering exercise, have students stay in a comfortable seat and imagine becoming more selfless with every exhale, and offering compassion and love to everyone around them with each exhale. Repeat this several times and allow them to reflect on how they feel after dedicating positivity to others.

Poses for Selflessness

Selflessness is represented by the *Warrior Poses*, which symbolize warriors who fight for the greater good and benefit of others. In particular, transitioning between *Warrior One* (Virabhadrasana I) into *Humble Warrior* (Baddha Virabhadrasana) can represent the strength that allows us to help others and our altruism and honor when we bow to others.

Furthermore, the *Splits* (Hanumanasana) represents selflessness because of the mythological story behind the pose. It is named after the god Hanuman, who took a giant leap over a large body of water to rescue a queen from an island that others could not reach—placing himself in danger and putting the queen's needs before his own.

More Inspiration on Selflessness

"Let us all dedicate our lives for the sake of the entire humanity. With every minute, every breath, every atom of our bodies we should repeat this mantra: 'dedication, dedication, giving, giving, loving, loving.'" – Swami Satchidananda

"Let your good deeds be like rain. Drop a little everywhere." — M. Nasiruddin Al-Albani

"Treat others as if they were what they ought to be and you help them become what they are capable of being." — Goethe

"No one needs love more than the person we find difficult to like." — Mike Moore

"The true meaning of life is to plant trees, under whose shade you do not expect to sit." — Nelson Henderson

"When given the choice between being right and being kind, choose kind." — Dr. Wayne Dyer

"People will forget what you said. People will forget what you did. But people will never forget how you made them feel." — Maya Angelou

"Before you speak, let your words pass through three gates: Is it true? Is it necessary? Is it kind?" — Rumi

- ♪ *Selfless* – The Strokes
- ♪ *Selfless* – Piotr Wiese
- ♪ *Devi Prayer* – Craig Pruess & Ananda

Notes

Understanding

Understanding is about accepting others as they are without judgment. It requires us to let go of stereotypes and preconceived notions by having an open mindset. It requires observing, listening, and a willingness to consider the world through alternative points of view. Understanding makes us kinder, wiser, and more appreciative of life.

Yoga represents the theme of understanding because the practice helps us to better understand ourselves and human nature. Yoga also incorporates the concept of *Ahimsa* which means non-judgment, including not comparing ourselves to others. Ahimsa also includes practicing kindness and compassion, which are essential for being open to understanding others.

Understanding as an Intention

Have students consider a time they wished they could have been more understanding of others, such as when they were quick to judge or made an unfair assumption. This could even relate to judging themselves. Then, encourage students to set an intention surrounding how they can be more understanding of others or possibly more understanding of themselves. Dedicate their practice to that person or group of people.

Centering for Understanding

Take *Akasha Mudra* (Touching the Void Gesture Gesture), which helps to free up space in the mind and rid of emotional waste and judgmental feelings of others. By clearing the mind, we can overcome preconceived notions in order to become more understanding and appreciative of others and ourselves.

> To take this mudra, touch the tips of the thumb and middle fingers together while keeping the palm facing upwards.

Consider having students repeat understanding-themed affirmations like the following:

> *I am an understanding person; I let go of judgment; I see myself in the position of others; I choose to see both sides*; etc.

A simple pranayama exercise can also be used as a centering technique for understanding. With each inhale, have students receive the ability to better understand others, and with each exhale, have students release all judgment of others. Repeat this for several rounds.

Poses for Understanding

Understanding can be represented by poses that are commonly made more comfortable with the use of props. This is because they also represent how yoga is about feeling rather than a shape. These kinds of poses allow us to be more mindful and understanding of ourselves and others.

For example, *Deer Pose* (Mrigiasana) represents the theme of understanding by highlighting differences in our hip anatomy, whereby our bone structure can determine how the hips internally and externally rotate. Thus, the pose can look different for everyone and often requires the use of blankets or bolsters to sit comfortably.

Furthermore, *Fire Log Pose* (Agnistambhasana) often feels more comfortable with the use of a bolster or blanket under the top knee to protect the joint. And sometimes yoga straps can forward folds. In all cases, these poses illustrate how yoga is about understanding what one's body needs in a particular pose at any given time. Thus, the use of props honors our unique anatomy.

Understanding is also represented by a *Standing Forward Bend* (Uttanasana). This simple forward fold helps us to understand where we experience tightness and the reasons that our bodies feel different at certain times—whether that is in the morning, after a workout, or after stretching. The pose also has several variations that can be taken depending on how the body feels, such as wrapping the hands around the calves to bend deeply or keeping a generous bend in the knees. The decision depends on our understanding of ourselves—which is a skill that can also help us understand others in our lives.

More Inspiration for Understanding

"You have to take people how they are because there are no others." – Konrad Adenauer

"Judging is preventing us from understanding a new truth. / Free yourself from the rules of old judgments and create the space for new understanding." – Steve Maraboli

"When a man points a finger at someone else, he should remember that four of his fingers are pointing at himself." – Louis Nizer

"An untroubled mind, no longer seeking to consider what is right and what is wrong, a mind beyond judgments, watches and understands." – Gautama Buddha

"If you judge people, you have no time to love them." – Mother Teresa

"No man should judge unless he asks himself in absolute honesty whether in a similar situation he might not have done the same." – Viktor E. Frankl

"Whilst performing asanas the yogi's body assumes many forms resembling a variety of creatures. His mind is trained not to despise any creature, for he knows that throughout the whole gamut of creation, from the lowliest insect to the most perfect sage, there breathes the same Universal Spirit, which assumes innumerable forms. He knows that the highest form is that of the Formless. He finds unity in universality." – B.K.S. Iyengar

- ♪ *Rain* – Robin Bennich
- ♪ *Infinite Sustain* – Amaranth Cove
- ♪ *Anyone Who Knows What Love Is (Will Understand)* – Irma Thomas

YOGA THEMES FOR MODERN YOGIS

Notes

CONCLUSION

"Yoga is an internal practice. The rest is just a circus"

— K. Pattabhi Jois

Inspiration for planning yoga classes is all around us, but not always easy to identify or encapsulate into a class theme. This book contributes toward the literature of yoga by helping to simplify the class planning process while accounting for the authentic personality and teaching style of every modern yoga practitioner. This objective is accomplished by offering guidance on personalizing classes through various centering techniques, themed intentions, and class preparation to personalize themed yoga classes. Moreover, this book contains fifty-two class themes to cover at least one comprehensive class plan for every week of the year. Within these themes, explanations, mindfulness practices, asana suggestions, and supportive material help to spark inspiration for planning meaningful and rewarding yoga classes for modern students of all backgrounds.

Eight themed chapters are included in this book that surround their own overarching topic of yoga class themes for modern yogis. This text includes a chapter on mindfulness themes that encourage students to be more appreciative of every moment. This book also includes themes relating to how we can appreciate the abundance that surrounds us every day. Other chapters provide class inspiration relating to invigoration and empowerment to embrace the best versions of ourselves. There is also a chapter on recognizing the infinite opportunities that are unique to everyone. Self-appreciation themes are also included to inspire more self-love through yoga. And other themes relate to self-discovery and the world beyond ourselves.

Each of these chapters and their combined fifty-two themes helps to provide a more enriching and rewarding yoga experience for students so that they might connect with yoga on a deeper and more profound level. The simplicity of these themes also reinforces how Westernized yoga can be experienced by everyone in this modern age—no matter their age, gender, race, or socioeconomic background.

This book provides straightforward and structured class themes, in addition to plenty of advice and inspiration to plan yoga classes that are catered to any day and mood. The content, including themes, chapter topics, suggested techniques, and guidance help to spark inspiration for a lifetime of rewarding and memorable yoga classes. This book ensures that you will never be stuck when planning a yoga class so that you can pay attention to what matters most as a yoga instructor—practice, play, and sharing the ancient tradition with others in our modern and complicated age.

To assist in putting these ideas into action, *Yoga Classes for Modern Yogis* also includes a dedicated introductory section addressing how to plan themed yoga classes by offering suggestions for centering, setting intentions, and class preparation that assist in making the class planning process easier and authentic to every teacher. This chapter also acts to spark additional curiosity for ongoing learning and practice.

Furthermore, this book concludes with some final tools for continued class planning. These additional resources include notes pages, workbook pages, references, further reading, and an index. In this regard, several blank pages are included to write down additional ideas relating to the contents of this book and any other ideas relating to modern yoga class themes. Use these pages to transfer class ideas, themes, and inspiration onto paper, and use these as a reference for planning future classes.

In addition, this book's several workbook pages can be used to bring your ideas to life. These include ten blank templates for brainstorming and planning additional themed yoga classes—enough to add an additional class theme to complement each chapter in this book, plus a couple of extra themes. These workbook pages also mirror the familiar structure of the fifty-two themes in this book to make the planning process straightforward.

CONCLUSION

The final pages of this book include references to books that were referred to when creating this book, and suggestions for additional reading. Furthermore, the index provided identifies pages with specific terminology and techniques, including poses, mudras, yogic concepts, and themes. The index also contains English and Sanskrit words, which is so important for modern yogis who use many of these translations interchangeably.

My hope is that the guidance and resources in this text will continue to inspire the yoga community to plan rewarding and thought-provoking yoga classes that have a positive and lasting impact on contemporary yogis. This ultimate goal can be achieved by theming and teaching yoga classes that embrace our differences while unifying us through common emotions and experiences. Rewarding classes consider the changing world around us and apply yoga as an instrument for better appreciating our lives as they evolve. As such, students can better connect to yoga, appreciate its teachings, and continue applying its philosophy after they roll up their yoga mats. Teaching carefully crafted themed yoga classes is an expression of modern love and respect that we can share to improve the lives of others and experience personal fulfillment.

Notes & Other Themes

NOTES & OTHER THEMES

YOGA THEMES FOR MODERN YOGIS

NOTES & OTHER THEMES

YOGA THEMES FOR MODERN YOGIS

NOTES & OTHER THEMES

Workbook Pages

Practice Theme
For Modern Yogis:

About
Overview & Significance:

Centering Techniques
Mudra; Affirmations; Meditation; Pranayama:

Practice Intention

Additional Inspiration
Quotes, Music, etc.

Complementary Poses

Practice Theme
For Modern Yogis:

About
Overview & Significance:

Centering Techniques
Mudra; Affirmations; Meditation; Pranayama:

Practice Intention

Additional Inspiration
Quotes, Music, etc.

Complementary Poses

Practice Theme
For Modern Yogis:

About
Overview & Significance:

Centering Techniques
Mudra; Affirmations; Meditation; Pranayama:

Practice Intention

Additional Inspiration
Quotes, Music, etc.

Complementary Poses

Practice Theme

For Modern Yogis:

About
Overview & Significance:

Centering Techniques
Mudra; Affirmations; Meditation; Pranayama:

Practice Intention

Additional Inspiration
Quotes, Music, etc.

Complementary Poses

WORKBOOK PAGES

Practice Theme
For Modern Yogis:

About
Overview & Significance:

Centering Techniques
Mudra; Affirmations; Meditation; Pranayama:

Practice Intention

Additional Inspiration
Quotes, Music, etc.

Complementary Poses

Practice Theme
For Modern Yogis:

About
Overview & Significance:

Centering Techniques
Mudra; Affirmations; Meditation; Pranayama:

Practice Intention

Additional Inspiration
Quotes, Music, etc.

Complementary Poses

WORKBOOK PAGES

Practice Theme
For Modern Yogis:

About
Overview & Significance:

Centering Techniques
Mudra; Affirmations; Meditation; Pranayama:

Practice Intention

Additional Inspiration
Quotes, Music, etc.

Complementary Poses

Practice Theme
For Modern Yogis:

About
Overview & Significance:

Centering Techniques
Mudra; Affirmations; Meditation; Pranayama:

Practice Intention

Additional Inspiration
Quotes, Music, etc.

Complementary Poses

Practice Theme
For Modern Yogis:

About
Overview & Significance:

Centering Techniques
Mudra; Affirmations; Meditation; Pranayama:

Practice Intention

Additional Inspiration
Quotes, Music, etc.

Complementary Poses

Practice Theme
For Modern Yogis:

About
Overview & Significance:

Centering Techniques
Mudra; Affirmations; Meditation; Pranayama:

Practice Intention

Additional Inspiration
Quotes, Music, etc.

Complementary Poses

References & Further Reading

Several foundational texts were referenced while completing this book. These sources are included here and categorized by the following topics: Asana, Mudras, Pranayama, and Theory & Spirituality. I recommend referencing these texts for further information and inspiration.

Pranayama

Light on Pranayama: The Definitive Guide to the Art of Breathing – B.K.S. Iyengar (2013)

Light on Yoga: The Bible of Modern Yoga – B.K.S. Iyengar (1995)

Mudras

Mudras for Modern Life: Boost your health, re-energize your life, enhance your yoga and deepen your meditation – Swami Saradananda (2015)

Mudras of India: A Comprehensive Guide to the Hand Gestures of Yoga and Indian Dance – Cain Carroll and Revital Carroll (2012)

Mudras Of Yoga: 72 Hand Gestures for Healing and Spiritual Growth – Cain Carroll (2013)

Asanas

Hatha Yoga Illustrated – Martin Kirk, Brooke Boon, Daniel Di Turo (2005)

The Complete Guide to Yin Yoga: The Philosophy and Practice of Yin Yoga – Bernie Clark and Sarah Powers (2019)

Teaching Yoga: Essential Foundations and Techniques – Mark Stephens and Mariel Hemingway (2010)

Asana, Pranayama, Mudra and Bandha – Saraswati Satyananda Swami (2008)

Science of Yoga: Understand the Anatomy and Physiology to Perfect Your Practice – Ann Swanson (2019)

Theory & Spirituality

Light on Life: The Yoga Journey to Wholeness, Inner Peace, and Ultimate Freedom – B.K.S. Iyengar (2006)

The Yoga Sutras of Patañjali – Swami Satchidananda (2012)

Index

A

afirmation, 172
afirmations, 26
agency, 151
asanas
   Adho Mukha
      Svanasana, 40, 43, 62, 80, 115, 132, 226
   Adho Mukha
      Vrksasana, 111, 143, 168
   Agnistambhasana, 240
   Alanasana, 92
   Ananda Balasana, 181
   Anjaneyasana, 92, 177
   Apanasana, 185
   Ardha Chandrasana, 143, 190
   Ardha Matsyendrasana, 173, 208
   Ardha Padmasana, 21
   Ardha Pincha
      Mayurasana, 43
   Baddha Konasana, 96, 101
   Baddha Virabhadrasana, 230, 237
   Bakasana, 51, 89, 108
   Balasana, 37, 40, 59, 62, 80, 128, 181, 198, 205
   Bharmanasana, 48, 115, 124, 131
   Bhujangasana, 80, 84, 226
   Bitilasana, 48
   Camatkarasana, 104
   Chakravakasana, 115, 194
   Chaturanga, 89, 132, 139, 167
   Dandasana, 20, 37, 55, 76, 111
   Eka Pada
      Rajakapotasana, 66, 73, 96, 160
   Garudasana, 51, 56, 163, 201
   Gomukhasana, 173
   Halasana, 111, 163
   Hanumanasana, 120, 143, 237
   Janu Sirsasana, 208
   Malasana, 88, 177, 218
   Mandukasana, 135
   Marjaryasana, 48
   Matsyasana, 194, 222
   Mayurasana, 108
   Mrigiasana, 240
   Natarajasana, 72, 84, 135, 194
   Navasana, 132, 152
   Padangusthasana, 51
   Padmasana, 21, 37, 47, 71, 72, 204
   Parivrtta Anjaneyasana, 92, 124
   Parivrtta Ardha
      Chandrasana, 144, 190
   Parivrtta Trikonasana, 124, 144, 160
   Parsva Bakasana, 160
   Parsva Balasana, 197
   Parsva Urdhva
      Hastasana, 147
   Parsvottanasana, 234
   Paschimottanasana, 76, 168
   Patita Tarasana, 104
   Phalakasana, 139, 164, 167

Prasarita Padottanasana I, 177
Purvottanasana, 139, 164
Salabhasana, 101, 194
Salamba Bhujangasana, 84, 222
Salamba Sarvangasana, 163
Salamba Setu Bandha Sarvangasana, 37
Samakonasana, 135
Savasana, 21, 37, 59, 62, 67, 96, 108, 128, 181, 185, 218
Setu Bandha Sarvangasana, 160, 185, 222
Shanti Virabhadrasana, 230
Siddhasana, 21, 37, 47
Simhasana, 101
Sirsasana, 43, 111, 143, 164, 168
Skandasana, 104, 177
Sukhasana, 20
Supta Baddha Konasana, 36, 59, 185
Supta Dandasana, 111, 163, 185
Supta Kapotasana, 96
Supta Matsyendrasana, 208
Supta Virasana, 36, 120
Svarga Dvijasana, 56, 88
Tadasana, 147, 174, 201
Tittibhasana, 108
Upavistha Konasana, 96
Urdhva Dhanurasana, 84, 135, 160
Urdhva Hastasana, 108, 147, 226
Urdhva Mukha Paschimottanasana, 152
Urdhva Mukha Svanasana, 80, 84, 194, 226
Urdhva Prasarita Eka Padasana, 190
Ustrasana, 124, 185, 194, 197
Utkata Konasana, 139, 177, 218
Utkatasana, 93, 108, 132, 201
Uttana Shishosana, 197
Uttanasana, 67, 76, 80, 84, 168, 240
Utthan Pristhasana, 66, 214
Utthita Hasta Padangustasana, 201, 230
Utthita Hasta Padangusthasana, 63
Utthita Parsvakonasana, 48, 156
Utthita Trikonasana, 124
Vajrasana/Bhujrasana, 21, 37
Vatayanasana, 139
Viparita Karani, 128
Viparita Virabhadrasana, 48, 205
Virabhadrasana, 92, 139, 234, 237
Virabhadrasana I, 204, 230, 237
Virabhadrasana II, 48, 205
Virabhadrasana III, 190
Virasana, 21, 36, 43, 120, 230
Vrischikasana, 51, 111, 143
Vrksasana, 51, 56, 139, 174, 181, 201, 226
Asteya, 200
authenticity, 176
awakening, 100
awareness. *See* consciousness

B

beauty, 71
Brahmacharya, 103

C

centering, 20
change, 110
class brainstorming, 16
class notes, 15

INDEX

class preparation, 29
confidence, 146
consciousness, 35
contentment, 75
courage, 119
creativity, 103
curiosity, 189

D

deceleration, 39
dream, 107
Drishti, 51, 56

E

ease, 42
equanimity, 46
expansiveness, 123
exploration, 155

F

forgiveness, 213

G

generosity, 217
gratitude, 79

H

habits, 142, 166
happiness. *See* joy
Hatha Yoga, 15
healing, 127
heart-opening, 193
honesty, 196

I

initiate. *See* awaken
inner-flame, 130
integrity, 200
intentions
    guiding students, 27
intuition, 114

J

journey, 159
joy, 83

L

life, 180
loving-kindness, 221

M

Maitri, 221
meditation, 23
    body scan, 23, 36, 66
    day trip, 72, 88, 108, 160
    home base, 51, 55, 152
    loving-kindness, 222
    memory trip, 76
    nature, 226
    sensory awareness, 23, 35, 36, 59, 190, 204
meta/metta, 221
mindfulness, 33
mudras, 21, 22
    Abhaya, 143

Abhaya Hrdaya, 138
Akasha, 22, 239
Anja, 51
Anjali, 22, 79, 200
Ardha Suchi, 135
Ashvaratna, 159
Bhairava, 62
Bhu, 172
Chin, 36, 163
Dhyana, 55
Ganesha, 146
Garuda, 155
Hakini, 189
Hamsasya, 92
Hridaya, 221
Jnana/Gyana, 22, 163, 207
Kaleswara, 166
Kali, 119
Karana, 151
Ksepana, 65
Kubera II, 107
Mahashirsha, 39
Matangi, 103
Matsya, 95
Mrit Sanjeevani, 184
Mushtika, 177
Padma, 72
Pitta Energizing, 127
Pralamba, 193
Prana, 180
Prithivi, 225
Sahasrara, 59
Samsti, 46
Sankalpa, 22, 87
Shakti, 110
Shankha Varta, 114

Shanmukhi, 204
Shikhara, 233
Shurkri, 229
Sukham, 42
Surya, 131
Tambula, 135
Udana, 83
Uttarabodhi, 100
Varada, 213, 236
Vishuddha, 197
Vistara, 123
Vyana, 76
Vyapak Anjali/
   Pushpaputa, 217

N

nature, 225
non-stealing, 200

O

opportunity, 149
optimism, 87
outlining classes, 29

P

patience, 134
peace, 229
perseverance, 138
perspective, 162
poses
   Accomplished/Sage,
     21, 47
   Aparigraha, 217
   Bird of Paradise, 56, 88
   Boat, 132, 152
   Bound Angle/Butterfly,
     96, 101
   Bridge, 160, 185, 222
   Camel, 124, 185, 194,
     197
   Candlestick, 111, 163,
     185
   Cat & Cow, 48, 115,
     194
   Cat Pulling its Tail, 208
   Center/Straddle Splits,
     135
   Chair, 93, 108, 132,
     201
   Child's Pose, 37, 40,
     59, 62, 80, 128,
     181, 198, 205
   Cobra, 80, 84, 226
   Corpse, 21, 37, 59, 62,
     67, 96, 108, 128,
     181, 185, 218
   Cow Face, 173
   cross legged position.
     See Easy Seat or
     Sukhasana
   Crow/Crane, 51, 89,
     108
   Dancer, 72, 84, 135,
     194
   Deer, 240
   Dolphin, 43
   Downward-Facing Dog,
     40, 43, 62, 80, 115,
     132, 226
   Dragon, 66, 96
   Eagle, 51, 56, 163, 201
   Easy Seat, 20
   Exalted/Reverse
     Warrior, 48, 205
   Extended Hand-to-Big-
     Toe, 201, 230
   Extended Puppy, 197
   Extended Side-Angle,
     48, 156
   Extended Triangle, 124
   Fallen Triangle/Star,
     104
   Figure-Four
     Stretch/Supine
     Pigeon, 96
   Fire Log, 240
   Fire Toes, 101
   Firefly, 108
   Fish, 194, 222
   Frog, 135
   Garland Pose/Yogi
     Squat, 88, 177, 218
   Goddess, 139, 177,
     218
   Half Lord of the Fishes,
     173
   Half Lotus, 21
   Half Moon, 143, 190
   Handstand, 111, 143,
     168
   Happy Baby, 181
   Headstand, 43, 111,
     143, 164, 168
   Head-to-Knee Forward
     Bend, 208
   Hero, 21, 37, 43, 120,
     230

INDEX

High Crescent Lunge, 92
High Plank, 139, 164, 167
Horse, 139
Humble Warrior, 230, 237
Kneeling, 21, 36
Legs Up-The-Wall, 128
Lion, 101
Locust, 101, 194
Lotus, 21, 37, 47, 71, 72, 204
Low Crescent Lunge, 92, 104, 177
Low Lizard, 66, 214
Low Plank, 89, 132, 139, 167
Lunge Twist, 92, 124
Mermaid, 73
Mountain, 147, 174, 201
Naughty Kitten, 115
One-Leg Baby Cradle, 181
Open Angle, 96
Peaceful Warrior, 230
Peacock, 108
Pigeon/Swan, 66, 96, 160
Plow, 111, 163
Pyramid, 234
Rag Doll, 67
Reclined Butterfly, 36, 59, 185
Reclined Hero, 36, 120
Reclined Hug, 185
Reclined/Supine Spinal Twists, 208
Sage, 37
Scorpion, 51, 111, 143
Seal, 84, 222
Seated Forward Bend, 76, 168
Seated Spinal Twists, 208
Seated Staff, 20, 21, 37, 55, 76, 111
Seated Twist, 173
Shoulder Stand, 163
Side Crow, 160
Side Lunge Pose, 177
Side Plank, 139
Sphinx, 222
Splits, 120, 143, 237
Standing Extended-Leg Stretch, 63
Standing Forward Bend, 67, 76, 80, 84, 168, 240
Standing Side Stretch, 147
Standing Split, 190
Supported Bridge, 37
Tabletop, 48, 115, 124, 131
Thread the Needle, 197
Toe Squat, 101
Toe Stand, 51
Tree, 51, 56, 139, 174, 181, 201, 226
Twisted/Revolved Half Moon, 144, 190
Twisted/Revolved Triangle, 124, 144, 160
Upward Plank, 139, 164
Upward Salute, 108, 147, 227
Upward-Facing Dog, 80, 84, 194, 226
Upward-Facing West Intense Stretch, 152
Warrior One, 204, 230, 237
Warrior Three, 190
Warrior Two, 48, 205
Warrior variations, 92, 139, 234, 237
Wheel/Upward Bow, 84, 135, 160
Wide-Legged Forward Bend, 177
Wide-Legged/Angle-Seated Forward Fold, 96
Wild Thing, 104
pranayama, 24
  box breathing, 135
  Kapalabhati (Breath of Fire), 25
  Nadi Shodhana (Alternate Nostril Breathing), 25, 47, 104, 167
  Sama Vritti (Equal Breathing), 24, 47

Simhasana Pranayama (Lion's Breath), 101, 147
Sitali (Cooling Breath), 25
Ujjayi (Victorious Breath), 24, 36, 92, 101, 139, 181, 226
Viloma (Breath Retention), 25, 42, 62, 96, 135
presence, 54
props, use of, 20, 37, 43, 67, 167, 173, 197, 218, 222, 240

R

recovery. *See* healing
references, 263
relationships, 233

Restorative Yoga, 15, 59, 66, 128

S

Santosha, 75, 79
Satya, 196, 200
selecting themes, 15
self-love, 184
serenity, 58
simplicity, 91
spaciousness, 95
special considerations, 30
stillness, 61
Sun Salutation, 40, 48, 80, 93, 226
surrender, 65
Surya Namaskar, 40, 48, 80, 93, 226

T

tuning-in, 203

U

understanding, 236, 239

V

Vinyasa Yoga, 15, 48, 84, 100

W

wisdom, 207

Y

Yin Yoga, 15, 61, 65, 66, 96, 208
Yoga Nidra, 108

About the Author

Madeline Kanuka McGee is a Certified Yoga Instructor, Author, and Professional Caddy living and teaching yoga between Vero Beach, Florida and Ireland's North West.

Madeline is a doctoral-level writer and law graduate with published work covering a range of topics from healthcare, drugs, and legal reform, to wartime mobilization and mass media. She studied Journalism as an undergraduate student before specializing in History and Political Science at McGill University, where she excelled in intensive research and analytical writing. Extending these skills, Madeline completed the JD program at Queen's University Belfast that supported her independent research interests in Medicines Law and her desire to live and work in Europe.

Madeline completed her 200-hour Hatha Yoga Teacher Training with Ulu Yoga in Thailand and Bali before becoming the Founder of Yoga By Madeline. She specializes in creative Vinyasa flows and enjoys exploring new challenges, themes, and intuitive movement through her yoga practice. For more information on Madeline's classes, lessons, events, publications, and online content, visit www.yogabymadeline.com and her social media platforms @yogabymadeline. For all inquiries related to this book, please contact media@yogabymadeline.com.

Printed in Great Britain
by Amazon